How to Sponsor a Minority Cultural Retreat

**The Human Relations
Activity of the Decade**

by Charles A. Taylor

D1401342

Published by Praxis Publications
P.O. Box 9869
Madison, WI 53715
608-244-5633

Library of Congress Cataloging-in-Publication Data

Taylor, Charles A. (Charles Andrew)
    How to sponsor a minority cultural retreat / by Charles A. Taylor.   p. cm.
    Includes bibliographical references.
    ISBN 0-935483-11-X : $24.95
        1. Intercultural education--United States. 2. Intercultural communication--United States. 3. Interpersonal relations.
I. Title.
LC1099.3.T39 1989
370.19'6--dc20   89-36895 CIP

___

Acknowledgements

Praxis Publications, Inc. gratefully acknowledges the following individuals for their contributions to the completion of this book.

Elizabeth Johanna, Chris Johns, Ingrid Maria Jimenez, Stephen Taylor, Michele Harper, Henry Villareal, Patricia Kelley Donsdatter

Illustrations by Monique J. Isham
Book design by Elizabeth Johanna

This book is dedicated to all those brave souls who are willing to risk vulnerability when reaching out across cultures.

___

© 1989 Praxis Publications, Inc.
Praxis Publications, Inc. is an independent Multicultural Business Enterprise which publishes educational and cultural literature and provides training programs, consultation and technical assistance to university and community groups. We invite you to call or write us for additional information about our services and products.

Meaning of Cover Illustration

In Ojibway tradition, the dreamcatcher is hung above a child's cradle. As the child dreams, the dreams float upwards. The good dreams flow through the center. The bad dreams are caught in the web. When the sun rises the bad dreams are burned off.

As illustrated in our book cover, we've adapted the dreamcatcher as a metaphor for the cultural retreat. By joining together as a group, participants can "catch" stereotypes, discrimination, incidents of racism, and see them for what they are and release them. Then, in unity they can let the strength of understanding flow through the center out into the world.

Foreword

This version of *How to Sponsor a Minority Cultural Retreat* reflects a number of changes from the original version - the *Cultural Retreat Handbook*. We have added new resources, new topics and reorganized the book in a way that is intended to improve the planning of your retreat.

Since writing the earlier version, I have had a chance to participate in and conduct additional retreats. As a result some modifications were made to the original text. Basically however, the book remains true to its original purpose; to share the Minority cultural retreat concept. While realizing that it is impossible to capture all of the dynamics that occur during this outing, it is possible to put together the format and objectives of such a gathering so that others can host retreats.

The more I read about the increasing number of racial incidents that are occurring on the nation's campuses and the more I travel, the more I am convinced of the importance of Minority cultural retreats. As one who has planned and participated in seminars, conferences and workshops, I know of no better method of piercing racial barriers than getting whites and people of color in a secluded setting and exposing them to issues that impact race and culture. Such exposure helps participants appreciate diversity and experience cultural pluralism first hand.

With this book, information is provided that is intended to help you duplicate a successful retreat. If you are interested in improving race relations or in getting individuals to broaden their perspectives, use this book to design your retreat. Then write me, because I want to know how you feel the retreat affected participants and what type of follow up occurred. Your feedback is important because as the retreat concept spreads, it will be good to network so that others can benefit from your experience.

Charles Taylor, author

CONTENTS

Introduction

Dear Mr. Taylor,

This was my first experience being involved in a cultural retreat. I've always been curious and respected other cultures than my own, but never really experienced it first hand. I've never lived with, or even near, people whose culture was not white. I've been acquainted with people of other cultures only on occasion.

I learned a lot over the weekend and feel that my values were strengthened, in regards to prejudice. I have always "stood up" for our so-called "minorities". I personally feel there are no minorities. As we learned, we are all one human race. I love to learn about people and find it was very important to learn about how other cultures live, communicate, believe, etc. All cultures should be respected for all the "good" they bring to our world. I think that if more people would shut their mouths and sit back and open their eyes and ears, they would see how much we are all " alike", no matter what color we are. That is what I learned this past weekend. What we experienced was real and it made me think a lot about my own values and beliefs. Ignorance is the key weakness of the "majority" and it could be turned into awareness if everyone would only care. I felt very ignorant most of the weekend, knowing very little about the tests we were given ... One thing I do know is that I intend to educate my children about other cultures than my own, and also to introduce them to children of other cultures to interact with. I received "no" education in regards to other cultures in school, church, or from my parents.

I think we have a lot of people to reach, but more and more people are becoming aware of the danger of prejudices. I have been telling a lot of people about my experience on the retreat and encouraging them to attend the (next) retreat. I feel that attitudes are so important when communicating to others. I intend to have a very positive attitude when it comes to talking to people about prejudices, discrimination, etc., emphasizing the fact that we are all "alike," even more so than I have done before! I feel I have more confidence now.

I think everyone had a great time too! I loved the great food, dancing and all the outdoors. It was a beautiful weekend all around. The speakers were really good . . . . I met some truly great people, people who got along just fine because we were ourselves - no hangups, no tensions, no discriminations! It's a good feeling to know that we all proved how much we are alike and I thank you for the opportunity to belong to that.

I think one of the speakers summed it up best when he said that if a force came from outer space, suddenly we would all become earthlings, one human race!

Crissy

Introduction

The preceding letter is one of many that I have received from participants over the years while conducting retreats. Although this particular letter was from a White participant, it is equally rewarding to hear how Black participants learn to appreciate American Indian Culture or other ethnic groups appreciate different cultures.

For the letter writer, the Minority Cultural Retreat experience had a profound impact. As one who has witnessed this impact time and time again, I felt it important that the cultural retreat concept be shared. Perhaps one of the reasons why a retreat is so successful is that it creates a forum for communication. It allows people to interact in a comfortable situation in which they can be themselves. The retreat gives people an opportunity to learn about minority cultures by experiencing, discussing and sharing it first hand. Minority Cultural Retreats introduce to participants selected aspects of the experiences of minority groups. They do not teach participants what it means to be Asian, Black, Hispanic or American Indian, but rather provide exposure to that reality.

Utilizing a structured approach, participants are engaged in sensitivity exercises, small group discussions and demonstrations to accomplish discovery and sharing. Disagreement and confrontation are treated as a natural consequence of cross cultural interaction, almost as prerequisites to honest interaction. Participants are told to channel their anger at issues rather than individuals. It is not uncommon for participants to question why they subjected themselves to this experience at the beginning of the retreat. Nor is it uncommon to hear comments like, "Do we really have to leave?" at the close of the retreat.

It is probably obvious by now that I am sold on the whole idea of retreats. A group of caring but skeptical people assemble themselves to dialogue over some of the most sensitive issues our society faces. At first they are really hesitant about what they say, being careful not to offend, but the structured activities slowly force them to be honest rather than tactful. When their honesty is not viewed in a judgmental way then genuine communication is possible. Perhaps two days is not long enough for lasting change, but it is time enough to create a foundation for change. Besides if we are not the generation that confronts racism and ethnocentrism squarely, than we have done a disservice to future generations.

In the pages ahead you will find information that should assist in making your retreat rewarding. Best wishes for a most successful experience.

CHAPTER 1

Although retreats are by no means limited to college students, the bulk of the Minority Cultural Retreat described in this book applies to retreats sponsored by college campuses. Community based organizations, churches, scouts and others should modify the information to meet your particular needs.

Planning Committee

A good planning committee is essential to a successful retreat. The following are general guidelines for the committee to consider.

1. Planning should begin at least four to six months before the retreat is scheduled to occur.

2. A committee of students, faculty and staff should plan the retreat.

3. A chairperson should be appointed early on, to take charge of the direction of the group, to help establish goals and to coordinate the committee's activities.

4. The committee must obtain financial support and commitment to ensure that the retreat will take place.

5. The committee needs to reserve its retreat site well in advance since such sites stay booked year round. Make sure the retreat site is secluded and far enough away from campus so that students cannot commute back and forth. Make sure the site has a large meeting room that will accommodate all the participants. Make sure that sleeping, bathing and eating facilities are adequate.

6. The committee should have sufficient contact with the speakers, presenters and entertainers to confirm goals of the retreat, what should be covered in the presentations and to determine miscellaneous things such as honorariums, equipment needs, handouts, etc.

7. The committee should pattern its agenda after the one included in this chapter.

8. The committee should make sure the check list on page 9 is completed prior to the retreat.

9. The committee should decide how the participants will be selected ensuring a good mix of White and Minority students.

What Is A Minority Cultural Retreat?

For our purposes, a Minority Cultural Retreat is a structured activity which allows Minority and non-Minority participants an opportunity to explore racial and cultural issues in a secluded setting that is free of major distractions. Participants who generally do not know each other are asked to spend two to three days eating, sleeping and working together. They are asked to literally submerge themselves in learning about minority cultures. Because of the time they are required to spend together, participants eventually "drop their guard" and allow their "true" feelings to surface. A seasoned facilitator will not only move this process along, she/he will also create an atmosphere where honest disclosure is expected. During the retreat participants are able to discuss, debate and contribute in ways that may help them discover, share and broaden their awareness of themselves in relationship to the multicultural world at large.

Activities, speakers and discussion groups focus on objectives which are designed to ensure that the experience participants are exposed to, challenge their beliefs, confront their values and require some type of follow up action.

A Minority Cultural Retreat, is designed to be informational and educational. Three aspects of culture are presented on each Minority group that is featured. 1) The cultural contributions (music, dance, art, etc.), 2) problems the group faces in contemporary American society, and 3) the group's U.S. and world history. The intent is to provide participants a context in which to understand the issues impacting a particular ethnic group.

The retreat experience is not designed to be complacent. It is dynamic and at times confrontational. However, as a result of such discourse, a certain bonding often takes place between participants. A sense of community among the participants frequently occurs. This process of permitting oneself to be vulnerable and open to new ideas often gives one an insight that results in increased cultural awareness. Comments like, "I had no idea . . .", are common during and after the retreat. Even the free time serves an important purpose during the retreat because participants are required to spend half of it with someone of a different racial group. When you consider the cultural activities, Minority speakers and the great outdoors, all these things contribute to making the retreat an effective human relations experience.

Since the real test of the retreat's effectiveness must occur after it is over, participants are expected to answer the question,

What Is A Minority Cultural Retreat?

"Where do we go from here?". They are expected to answer this question individually and collectively through small groups.

Minority Cultural Retreats will not solve racial problems in our society or on our campuses and that is not their intent. However, they do provide people the opportunity to explore racial and cultural similarities and differences. Perhaps our of this exploration may come the willingness to find out more, to work together and to strive for a world that respects the cultural heritage and uniqueness of all of its inhabitants.

If the retreat is able to achieve that, then the potential impact it can have on race relations may make it the human relations activity of the '90's.

Publicity

Like any event in which you are trying to attract participants, it is necessary to get the word out. Publicity should begin at least two months before the retreat takes place. The important point to consider is to make sure you use your theme in all of your publicity so that potential attendants begin to identify the theme with the event. We recently used a catchy theme that was written like this: **D**n*versity* which meant unity through diversity at the university. The T-shirts we distributed had the theme written on them as well as press releases, flyers, posters and handouts. The theme created enough curiosity to ensure student interest. It also reinforced the retreat's objectives.

Selecting Participants

If this is your first retreat, it is recommended that you limit participation to White and Minority student leaders. Future retreats will not need to be restricted as such. This recommendations is made because if you can get your student leadership to interact cross culturally, the pay off for the campus can be tremendous. If successful you will have also put together a support group of influential individuals who will help keep the need to improve race relations alive throughout the year. Student leaders are in a position to implement follow up activities and invigorate their membership to strive for a real change in racial attitudes on campus. The birth of a multicultural student organization has occurred on some campuses as a result of having student leadership participate in the first retreat.

In addition to sending written invitations to student organizations, nothing beats a personal approach. Members of the planning committee (which should include student leaders) should get on student groups' agendas and talk about the retreat and

Selecting Participants

recruit members in person. After the personal appeals have been made a formal written invitation with a confirmation slip should be sent. This may need to be followed with phone calls. This may seem like overkill, but the care you devote to the selection of participants will help them appreciate the importance of this event and may make them feel apart of something that is pioneering.

Key consideration must also be given to racial and sexual representation. Ideally the planning committee would want an equal number of males and females, Minorities and Whites. To achieve this mix, more than likely you will need to manipulate your enrollment. This can be done a number of ways. For example you can limit enrollment to twenty students from white students organizations and twenty to organizations represented by students of color, with the stipulation that both sexes are to be equally represented. It is best to limit the size of the group between 30 and 50 people. If you are at a campus with few student organizations or Minority groups, modify the representation accordingly or invite students from nearby campuses.

Once a participant list has been compiled and confirmed (that includes the race and sex of each participant) you can then begin to do some ethnic pairing on paper. You can assign roommates in advance. We recommend that you assign participants certain colors on their name tags for group work assignments. You can assign "seatmates" for the bus activity on the way to the retreat site, etc. It is probably good to have a participant waiting list because invariably someone will cancel out at the last minute.

The Facilitator

It is vital that the person selected to facilitate the retreat be a sensitive and culturally aware individual. Although there will probably be a number of speakers giving presentations throughout the retreat, it will still be the facilitator's role to guide the retreat in such a manner that it ends up being a positive structured experience for the participants. As a result we recommend that you select a facilitator based on the following characteristics:

1. He/She permits all group members to express their opinions.

2. He/She gives equal status to opinions expressed and does not attempt to stifle dissent.

3. He/She views his/her role as supportive and views the retreat from a holistic point of view.

The Facilitator

4. He/She needs to be well organized to ensure the event moves along with few as possible interruptions, but flexible enough to allow for spontaneity.

5. He/She is able to personalize his/her interaction with the participants, joins in when appropriate and is at ease on a first name basis with the participants.

6. He/She is able to mediate disputes and seek compromises when necessary.

7. He/She is able to be assertive without being dictatorial.

Trouble Shooter

A trouble shooter should always be available to handle last minute emergencies that tend to arise even with the best laid plans. This person should stay in constant communication with the facilitator and presenters making sure that all equipment needs are met. A car should be at his/her disposal as well as $20-$50 in petty cash for miscellaneous expenses.

Head Cabin Mates

It is important that a designated individual serve as the contact person in the male and female sleeping quarters to handle concerns, enforce quiet hours and assume general responsibility.

Presenters

Presenters can make or break a retreat. Keeping in mind the topics to be covered along with the objectives you are trying to accomplish, select presenters who can handle both professionally, and in a manner that moves participants intellectually and emotionally.

Bus Activity

All participants should travel to the retreat on the bus together and at least one staff person should drive a car for use in emergencies. Prior to boarding the bus, briefly assemble the participants and give them each a number or color. Have them pair up with the person with the same number or color. (It should be obvious that how the numbers or colors were distributed was predetermined from your confirmed participant list.) Tell them they are to sit with this person on the ride to the retreat site. Instruct them to complete the following activities prior to arrival at the retreat site. (Be sure to provide pencils and paper and the information starred below.)

Each person is to interview their seatmate obtaining the following information:

Bus Activity

*name and/or nickname; ethnic/racial background; job; year in school; major; travel and hobbies/interests.

*why they signed up for the retreat.

*describe their first experience with someone who was racially different.

*one thing (activity, food, sports) they like and one thing they dislike.

*have them demonstrate something from their culture (ie hand shake, hand game, how to comb hair) that involves touch.

The objectives for the bus activity includes:

a) Getting students to communicate cross culturally from the outset.

b) Allowing students to meet on a personal basis and use the information gained from the interview to introduce the student to the group later during the opening ceremonies.

c) preventing students from grouping by race or forming cliques.

d) Creating a situation where participants are expected to touch.

It has been our experience that some participants have never physically touched someone who is ethnically different. The mere act of touching often refutes stereotypes one has.

Arrival

Once you arrive at the campsite your primary consideration is room assignments if you didn't pre-assign roommates prior to boarding. To maximize the cultural experience we suggest room assignments be based on ethnic differences. Mix participants up. The easiest method is to assign roommates in advance based on your pre-enrollment. You can also assign participants certain numbers or colors and combine numbers or colors as roommates. Just make sure you distribute the numbers or colors in a way that ensures white and minority interaction/pairing.

Tour of the Retreat Site

After the group has unloaded its gear we recommend that you take everyone on a tour of the campsite. This helps participants become familiar with their surroundings quickly. Signs around the retreat site that say, "Welcome to the Cultural Retreat," tend to reassure participants. It's a good idea to show participants where the hiking trails, and swimming areas are located.

Cultural Retreat Objectives and Expectations

It is important to establish clear and do-able objectives because they determine to a large extent the structure of your program. Activities and exercises should be planned around your objectives. Feel free to use some or all of our suggested objectives below.

The following are suggested as objectives and expectations for the retreat experience. Participants are expected to:

1. Increase awareness and heighten sensitivity to minority cultures.

2. Experience selected aspects of minority cultures.

3. Gain experience in completing projects, discussions, etc., together as a group.

4. Broaden their awareness of themselves in relationship to the multicultural world at large.

5. Take risks in expressing their opinions and ideas through honest self-disclosure.

6. Explore minority cultural values.

7. Confront personal prejudices.

8. Analyze personal historical responsibilities.

9. Share their cultural interests and feelings with the group.

10. Identify strategies that would help promote cultural pluralism.

11. Reaffirm our commonly shared humanity.

12. Explore differences and similarities between cultures.

13. Plan some type of individual follow-up from their retreat experience.

Costs

Ideally, if you have a budget from which you can finance the costs of the retreat, it should be free to participants. If you do not, the budget below provides some general guidelines to estimate costs. This budget is based on participants spending two nights and three days at the retreat.

Retreat Budget

Site (lodging) 50 people x $20/person	$1,000.00
Food	500.00
Transportation	250.00
Honorariums/Ethnic Entertainment	600.00
Packets for Participants	50.00
T-Shirts	300.00
Publicity	25.00
Equipment Rental	75.00
Misc. Supplies	75.00
Total Estimated Budget	$2,875.00

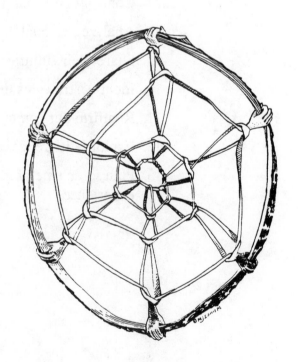

Check List

> The planning committee should make sure that the following items on the retreat check list are completed prior to the event taking place.

____Identify, reserve and checkout the retreat site.

____Agree upon the retreat date.

____Identify the funding to pay for the retreat.

____Select participants to attend and have them return confirmation slips.

____Agree upon a theme for the retreat.

____Identify speakers, presenters and amount of honorariums.

____Send letters to speakers, presenters and identify equipment needs.

____Identify films, videos and cultural entertainment for participants.

____Design, layout and print agenda.

____Publicize retreat.

____Determine the ethnic menus and recipes.

____Reserve transportation to and from site.

____Identify a driver whose car is available for errands or emergencies.

____Determine what should be included in the retreat packets.

____Put together and bring retreat packets.

____Determine free time activities.

____Determine who will serve as the "trouble shooter," facilitator and head cabin mates during the retreat.

____Finalize retreat rules.

____Send invitations to the campus administration.

____Order T-shirts for distribution at retreat M, L and XL sizes.

____Create check-in form to check-in participants on the bus for both departures.

Planning Your Retreat

Check List

_____Determine departure site and time.

_____Have Participants sign hold harmless agreement for liability
      purposes.

_____Make sure you have adequate insurance coverage. (Many
      university insurance policies automatically cover this activity).

_____Obtain Maps of the retreat site.

_____Give participants a "what to bring" sheet.

_____Create an evaluation form for the retreat.

_____Bring ethnic music to play during the retreat.

_____Determine bus trip activity.

_____Bring camera, film, tape recorder, video cassette recorder,
      TV monitor, extension cords and adapters.

_____Bring pots, pans, utensils, napkins, dish rags, detergent,
      soap, extra toiletries.

_____Bring food if you are cooking your own; other wise snacks.

_____Bring sports and recreational items. (i.e. football, volleyball,
      horseshoes, etc.)

_____Bring a junk box with tape, pencils, paper, scissors, etc.

_____Determine who will be responsible for various aspects of the
      Agenda

Cultural Retreat Rules

> These rules should be read during the orientation. Every one is expected to abide by them.

1. Everyone is required to attend all sessions and be on time.

2. (Optional if applicable) Men will be responsible for kitchen duties on Friday, women on Saturday. Everyone is responsible for Sunday's kitchen duties.

3. Sleeping quarters close at (fill in time) and quiet hours begin.

4. Be sure to read over any specific rules that the camp ground may require (i.e. no firearms, alcohol, drugs, TVs or pets).

5. Use a "buddy system" for hiking, boating, swimming and whenever someone is leaving the cabin at night. If a black-board is available it can be used as a way of keeping track of who is out of the cabin and when she/he is expected back.

6. Go over procedures you have established to handle sickness or emergencies. Bring along a first aid kit.

7. Go over the four cultural practices that all participants must abide by. (See page 16)

8. Remind participants that half of their free time must be spent with a person of a different racial group.

9. Make additional assignments (to build campfires, and to assist retreat coordination in miscellaneous activities) as needed.

10. Prohibit smoking during the sessions.

11. Remind everyone, whether they agree or not, to respect one another's opinion.

12. Remind people not to engage in put downs during the retreat. Constructive feedback is welcomed as long as it does not threaten anyone individually. Attack the issues, not the person.

13. Inform the group they will need to plan some type of individual follow-up from their retreat experience.

14. Have participants leave the retreat site cleaner than they found it.

Agenda To Use For Your Retreat

It is a good idea to go over the agenda in detail. Always start on time. Although some of the activities may go over the allotted time, when possible stay on schedule. This reduces the problem of stragglers later on. Be sure each person has an agenda and retreat packet that includes pencils, papers and pertinent information.

The agenda that follows is one that we have successfully on past retreats. You can substitute any ethnic group into a particular time slot. This agenda can be lengthened if you have other ethnic groups, you want to include, or shortened as appropriate.

The agenda decribes our most common retreat featuring Native American, African American and Hispanic American culture. Although Asian Americans are not included, they can be. To add any other culture, you simply need to provide three hours and forty-five minutes in the agenda. This can be done by starting the retreat earlier on Friday.

Also, be sure to assign responibility for the activities on the agenda. This helps assure a successful program.

Small group discussions proved to be very productive

Minority Cultural Retreat Agenda

Day One

	Activity	Time

Person(s) Responsible (You will need to assign a person to be responsible for each activity listed.)	1. Departure from Campus
	   a) Check-In of Students
	   b) Bus Activity
		2:30 pm

	2. Arrive at Campsite
	   a) Unpacking/Settling In
	   b) Tour of Campsite
		3:30 pm

	3. Introduction/Orientation
	   a) Introductions/Ice Breakers
	   b) Overview of Retreat
	   c) Explanation of Rules/Objectives
		4:15 pm

	4. Presentation on Native American Culture	5:00 pm
	5. Native American Supper	6:30 pm
	6. Native American Culture and Entertainment	7:30 pm
	7. Break	8:45 pm

	8. Small Group Sessions
	   a) Reaction to Native American Culture Presentation
	   b) Discussion of problems minority students face on campus.
		9:00 pm

	9. Free Time	10:30 pm
	10. Quiet Time	11:30 pm

Minority Cultural Retreat Agenda

Day Two

Person(s) Responsible	Activity	Time
	11. Breakfast/Free Time	7-8:15 am

	12. Seminar
	  a) Warm Up Activity
	  b) Showing and discussion of video "Racism 101"
	  c) Break
	  d) Student Panel and Reactions
		8:30 am

	13. Free Time	11:30 am
	14. Lunch/Free Time	12:30 pm
	15. Presentation on African American Culture	1:30 pm
	16. Free Time	3:00 pm
	17. African American Culture and Entertainment	4:00 pm
	18. Reactions to African American Presentation	5:30 pm
	19. Supper Featuring Soul Food and Free Time	6:15 pm
	20. Group Project: Where do we go from here?	7:15 pm
	21. Soul Dance, Social Time, Free Time	8:45 pm
	22. Quiet Time	12:00 am

Minority Cultural Retreat Agenda

Day Three

Person(s) Responsible	Activity	Time
	23. Breakfast/Free Time	7:30 am
	24. Cultural Exploration Activity	8:30 am
	25. Presentation on Hispanic Culture	9:00 am
	26. Break	10:30 am
	27. Hispanic Culture and Entertainment	10:45 am
	28. Hispanic Lunch/Free Time	12:15 pm
	29. Reactions to Hispanic Culture Presentation	1:15 pm
	30. Follow Up Activities (Where Do We Go From Here?)	2:00 pm
	31. Closing Ceremony	3:00 pm
	32. Departure from retreat site	3:45 pm

Explanation of Agenda (Numbers correspond with the numbers used in the agenda.)

Day One

1. Departure
    This has been previously covered under the section Bus Activity. See page 5.

2. Arrival
    This is covered on page 6.

3. Introduction/Orientation
    This segment of the retreat is very important. It sets the stage for the entire activity. It is best to have participants sitting in a circle in chairs or on the floor - remember you are at a campsite in blue jeans. Casual clothing is highly recommended. Formal attire should be discouraged. The intent is to create a comfortable relaxed environment. During the introductions have the bus seatmates introduce each other using the information they gathered during the interview, on the bus ride to the retreat site. Then have each person tell why they came, what they hope to get out of the retreat and what they plan on doing with the information they will acquire. Video tape this if possible for playback during the closing ceremony. Next, go over the purposes, expectations and rules of the retreat. We have provided a list of rules that were used on past retreat. We have also listed several introductory exercises that can be used.

    There are four cultural practices that should be used throughout the retreat.

a. Everyone must use the Spanish word "hola" (which means hello) when greeting on another.

b. Everyone that shakes hands must use a national black handshake! (see side bar)

c. Whenever possible sit in a circle to honor the Native American tradition in which a circle represents the circle of life and unity.

d. Any disputes or arguments are to be settled with the traditional Asian bow to restore respect, show humility and honor! (optional) You may substitute this with a peace tent in which those with strong disagreements can enter but not leave until the dispute has been resolved, even if the dispute ends with agreeing to disagree.

National Black Handshake

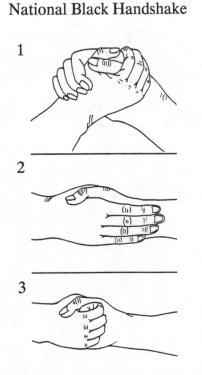

1

2

3

16

Explanation of Agenda

4. Presentation on Native American Culture

Presenter(s) should address three aspects of Indian culture. 1) Cultural contributions, (music, dance, art, etc.), 2) problems the group faces in American society, and 3) and overview of the group's U.S. and world history. Be sure to have the presenters leave time for questions and answers. One activity that has proven effective (in setting a context for the speaker's remarks) is to quiz participants with an ethnic history test prior to the presentation. Samples of such tests are located in chapter four.

It is our belief that the experts of a culture must come from within the culture. Therefore we strongly recommend the presentor or speaker be a member of that minority group. This person should be knowledgable about the culture, language, contributions and struggles his/her group has experienced in American society. In many cases this person is providing participants with their first significant exposure to minority culture.

5. Native American Supper

Plan to serve one ethnic meal for each minority group being discussed at the retreat. If possible have the preparation of the meal be a lesson by having participants help prepare the meals. Be sure to include recipes for all the ethnic meals in the retreat folders. Recipes can be found in the addendum.

6. Native American Culture and Entertainment

Some aspect of music, dance, or art should be presented here. We have experienced much success with presentations on the "meaning of the drum", Native American dances and mini pow wows.

7. Break

This is a brief fifteen minute break.

8. Small Group Sessions
   a) Reactions to Native American Culture

Participants should be divided into small groups between five and seven people. If you can color code (two to three colors) your name tags in advance you can ensure that your groups are represented racially and by gender. You then can simply have the "blues" form a group, the "reds" etc. Have the groups discuss their reactions to the presentation on Native American culture.

The following questions may help stimulate the discussion: What did you learn about the culture that you previously didn't know? What sticks out in your mind most about what was

Explanation of Agenda

presented? How has your perception of Native Americans changed as a result of this presentation? What do you plan to do differently, if anything, with the information you have been exposed to?

b. Discussion of Problems Minority Students Face On Campus (Instructions for this activity are found in the addendum)

After getting students reactions to the presentation have the groups discuss problems Minority Students face on campus. You may want to form new groups so that people have a chance to work with many different people during the retreat. Each group/ committee selects a spokesperson to report its findings and proposed solutions on Day Two to representatives of the campus administration. This involves a brainstorming and listing of ideas. Each group should narrow the list to the top three problems. Representatives of the campus administration should be invited. This provides the students with an opportunity for feedback. If there are no administrative representatives available, a meeting should be planned with the administration once students return to campus. This lends credibility to this activity by ensuring that problems identified will be presented to the administration.

9. Free Time

The important thing to remember at free time is that half of a person's free time must be spent with a person of a different ethnic/racial group. For the most part free time activities should be left unstructured. However it is helpful if free time activities include Minority related games and activities, ethnic films, etc. Free time is a great time to offer group activities. Additionally if you are at a campsite, canoeing, volleyball, horseshoes, football, and nature trips are excellent group activities. It is still hard to beat a campfire, stories and music.

10. Quiet Time

Be sure to mention that participants are to respect everyone's right to a full night's sleep.

Explanation of Agenda

11. Breakfast/Free Time

Since participants wake up at different times, it is convenient to have at least an hour reserved for breakfast. Those who eat early should be encouraged to use their free time meeting someone new. It is not necessary that breakfast be ethnic.

12. Seminar
   a. Warm Up Activity

This activity is designed to start the day off right and help prepare students for the activities that follow. Examples of warm up activities are located in chapter 4.
   b. Discussion of Video "Racism 101"

This is an excellent video that explores some of the racist incidents that have been occurring on college campuses. It is a candid look from various perspectives of race relations on campus. It is approximately an hour long. Leave ample time for discussion, because after watching this, students generally have plenty to say. There are discussion questions in the addendum that can be used after showing the video.
   c. Break
   d. After the break, have the spokespersons who were selected on Friday night (to present to representatives of the campus administration) form a panel. Each member of the panel should be allowed a few minutes to present her/his findings. After the panel has presented, allow representatives from the campus administration a chance to respond. Allow ample time for questions and answers. If there are no administrative representatives present, have the panel present its findings to the participants allowing ample discussion. The discussion can be used to further focus the recommendations that can be presented to the campus administration once the students return to campus.

13. Free Time

(follow same procedures as before)

14. Lunch/Free Time

Again there is no need to be ethnic for lunch.

15. Presentation on African American Culture

Follow the same procedures used for Native American culture.

Explanation of Agenda

16. Free Time
   More free time is built into the schedule on Saturday. If the weather is nice, this really enhances the interpersonal relationships you are trying to foster.

17. African American Culture and Entertainment
   Follow same procedures used for Native American culture and entertainment. African American dancers, theater troups and musicians have been used successfully.

18. Reaction to African American Presentation
   Follow same procedures used in the reaction to Native American Culture.

19. Supper Featuring Soul Food/Free Time
   Recommended menu is located in the addendum.

20. Group Project: Where do we go from here?
   (Instructions for this activity are found in the addendum) Divide participants into small groups of five to seven members. Have them brainstorm what their group will do as a follow up from this experience. After they have compiled a list, have them narrow it down to one to three activities they pledge to pursue once they return to campus. Have them select a spokesperson for the group. The spokesperson will share the groups pledge during the follow up activity session on Day Three. A recorder should write down the group's pledges. Also each participant is to come up with at least one follow up activity that he/she plans to fulfill. Individual pledges need not be discussed during the group sessions but each participant will be asked to share them during the closing ceremony.
   This session is very important. It gives students a chance to be personally involved in not only identifying the problem, but working toward solutions. Perhaps of more importance is that usually students pledge to continue to meet after the retreat is over, thus ensuring long range benefits.

21. Soul Dance, Social Time, Free Time
   This is the time for students to relax and enjoy themselves. Have someone teach the participants the latest soul dances and have participants share dances from their particular culture.

22. Quiet Time

Explanation of Agenda

> Day Three

23. Breakfast/Free Time

24. Cultural Exploration Activity
    See chapter 4 for an activity to conduct here. Warm up activities can be used instead, depending on the mood of the group.

25. Presentation on Hispanic Culture
    Follow the same procedure used with the other cultures.

26. Break

27. Hispanic Culture and Entertainment
    Follow the same procedures used for Native American Culture and Entertainment.

28. Hispanic Lunch/Free Time
    (See Addendum for Mecican food recipes).

29. Reactions to Hispanic Culture Presentation
    Follow the same procedures used in reactions to Native American Culture.

30. Follow-Up Activities
    Appoint a recorder to write down the groups pledges. Have each spokesperson report to the total group what her/his group pledges to do as a follow up from the retreat. Leave ample time for discussion and encourage participants to agree on some type of self-monitoring so that their pledges actually get acted upon.

31. Closing Ceremony
    Give each participant a chance to tell what he/she acquired over the weekend. If you video taped the orientation, play back participants comments on what they had hoped to get out of the retreat and discuss. Some people like to have students complete their evaluations here. You can do so while the retreat is fresh in their minds or you can mail it to them later. A sample evaluation form is provided on page 24. Next have students form a large circle. Have all join hands and have each cite their personal method of following up on the retreat.

32. Departure
    Tell participants to leave the campsite better than they found it.

Planning Your Retreat

Follow-Up Activities

> When carried out successfully the cultural retreat helps to improve race relations and foster cross cultural communication. To keep the momentum alive participants are asked to develop individual and group follow up activities. Below we have listed follow up activities that were generated from past retreats.

Have participants write an essay describing their experiences and what they learned about other cultures for class credit or for the campus newspaper.

Have them write a letter describing their feelings about the retreat experience and then mail the letters to them a month later. Have them respond to what they had previously written.

Follow up with a one day urban retreat to a minority community providing students with "real life" cultural exposure.

Sponsor a community pot luck with ethnic dishes and show slides of the retreat experience.

Set up a cultural swap shop to exchange different types of cultural information.

Conduct some cultural games with various campus organizations sending representatives to compete.

Sponsor a Mini-Course on the cultural retreat experience.

Encourage the participants to communicate with a new person they met at the retreat at least once a month.

Create a retreat advisory committee to help plan the next one.

Make names, addresses and phone numbers of all participants available (by consent only) to all attendants for future getting together.

Host cross cultural exchanges, ethnic dinners, panel discussions, workshops, and cultural games.

Sponsor programs to expose the majority to contemporary problems faced by minority groups.

Create support networks (interact with minority groups around the area); form a friendship league, host a mix and match night, or a brotherhood and sisterhood week.

Follow Up Activities

Plan out-reach programs, minority parents weekend; Minority Alumni day, get acquainted day, tours to ethnic communities.

Sponsor presentations such as Black author of the month discussions, brown bag seminars, and multicultural arts festivals.

Sponsor a T-shirt day in which participants wear the T-shirts that were distributed at the retreat and hold a rap session.

Provide minority student leadership training so that minority students can assume leadership roles on campus.

Plan motivation activities such as recognition nights, contests on Black history themes, women's issues, campus radio programs, and campus bulletin board displays.

Place cultural cards, calendars, and minority related information on student union tables.

Promote involvement with student government and encourage them to sponsor multiracial seminars.

Outdoor activities foster student interaction

Minority Cultural Retreat Evaluation Form

> We would like your feedback on the effectiveness of this retreat. Please take a few minutes and complete this evaluation form by answering every item. Thank you.

check one

1. Sex   __M   __F

2. Ethnicity

__Black   __Hispanic   __White

__Native American   __Asian   __Other

3. Year in School

__Fr   __So   __Jr   __Sr   __Grad   __Other

How would you rate the following: (please circle your answer)
Circle N/A only if you did not attend the activity.

Day One	N/A	Poor	Fair	Good	Excellent
4. Bus Trip Activities	0	1	2	3	4
5. Friday Orientation Session	0	1	2	3	4
6. Native American Supper	0	1	2	3	4
7. Native American Cultural Presentation	0	1	2	3	4
8. Native American Entertainment	0	1	2	3	4
9. Reactions to Native American Culture	0	1	2	3	4
10. Small Group Discussion of Problems Minority Students Face on Campus	0	1	2	3	4

11. Comments on any of Day One's activities.

Minority Cultural Retreat Evaluation Form

Day Two	N/A	Poor	Fair	Good	Excellent
12. Warm Up Activity	0	1	2	3	4
13. Discussion of Video "Racism 101"	0	1	2	3	4
14. Discussion with representatives of the campus administration	0	1	2	3	4
15. African American Cultural Presentation	0	1	2	3	4
16. African American Culture/Entertainment	0	1	2	3	4
17. Reactions to African American Culture	0	1	2	3	4
18. Soul Food Supper	0	1	2	3	4
19. Small Group Discussion Where do we go from here?	0	1	2	3	4
20. Soul Dance, Social Time	0	1	2	3	4

21. Comments on any of Day Two's activities.

Day Three	N/A	Poor	Fair	Good	Excellent
22. Warm Up Activity Cultural Exploration Activity	0	1	2	3	4
23. a. Hispanic Culture Presentation	0	1	2	3	4
b. Hispanic Lunch	0	1	2	3	4
24. Hispanic Entertainment	0	1	2	3	4
25. Reactions to Hispanic Culture	0	1	2	3	4
26. Follow Up Session	0	1	2	3	4
27. Closing Ceremony	0	1	2	3	4

28. Comments on any of Day Three's Activities

Minority Cultural Retreat Evaluation Form

29. How did you feel about the arrangements for:

	N/A	Poor	Fair	Good	Excellent
Sleeping	0	1	2	3	4
Meeting	0	1	2	3	4
Recreational	0	1	2	3	4
Free Time	0	1	2	3	4
Dining	0	1	2	3	4
Transportation	0	1	2	3	4

30. Do you believe the retreat met its stated objectives? ___Yes ___No
    If no, why not?

31. Was the retreat well organized? ___Yes ___No
    If no, why not?

32. Do you believe that retreats like this should be held in the future?
    ___Yes ___No If no, why not?

33. Was the time of year suitable for the workshop? ___Yes ___No If no,
    when would be a better time?

34. Was there enough publicity generated about the retreat? ___Yes ___No

35. Please comment on the length of the sessions. Were they too short? Too
    long? Just right?

36. What was the highlight of the experience for you?

37. What was the low point?

38. If you could change one thing about the retreat, what would it be?

39. Would you be willing to be involved in the planning of future retreats?
    ___Yes ___No If yes, please leave your name and address when you turn
    in this evaluation form.

40. Over all comments.

Please return to _____ by _____.
                        name   date

CHAPTER 2

Introduction

Much of the history describing the relationship between white ethnics and People of Color is a record of broken promises, racial discrimination and a "trail of tears". Racial minorities in America have been dispossessed, enslaved, invaded and segregated.

The contributions they have made to American society have been largely ignored. Contemporary history courses still proclaim Columbus as the "discoverer" of America. Students are seldom taught that Spanish settlements thrived in New Mexico, Arizona and California long before the English colony of Jamestown was founded. The enormous wealth generated from slave labor permitted the capitalistic system to survive, while the sweat and blood of Chinese workers helped to bring the east and west together by laboring for the transcontinental railroad.

From slavery to anti-immigration laws, the experience of racial minorities in America has been one of oppression and discrimination. It was only in this century that Native Americans became U.S. citizens. Less than forty-five years ago Japanese were put in concentration camps in this country. The Civil Rights Act of 1964 and the Voting Rights Act that followed took place only twenty-five years ago granting Blacks and other disenfranchised groups the promise of a better America.

To be sure, progress has occurred in the society in the past thirty years, but it is generally accepted that this progress, has occurred in the political arena with the passage of laws. Less progress is evident in the economic realm. The economic gap between Whites and the rest of the population (especially Blacks, Native Americans and Hispanics) continues to widen to the point where economists refer to innercity racial minority communities as "permanent under class". The depravation, crime and assorted social ills associated with those communities are not seen as a by product of what the Kerner commission called institutional racism, but rather as evidence that racial minorities deserve their status in the society.

The unequal treatment minority groups experienced historically has greatly influenced how they view the society. This experience helps explain why their perceptions in many cases are substantially different from their white counterparts. While many Whites believe that the government has done enough for minority groups and that programs like Affirmative Action threaten their own interests, it is safe to say that most minority groups feel that not enough has been accomplished for the government to wash its

Introduction

hands. The period of benign neglect and outright hostility to minority aspirations, that seemed to characterize the Reagan era tended to confirm minority group fears that they could never take their hard won rights for granted.

The widespread support of Reagan's agenda and his immense popularity among white ethnics did little to improve race relations in the country. Racial incidents increased throughout the Reagan era. The Reagan legacy continues with recent Supreme Court decisions that attack Affirmative Action programs that make it more difficult for minority groups to prove discrimination in the work force. It should be understandable that a good deal of discontent exists when people of color compare their educational, housing, employment, health, economic, political and social status to that of white ethnics. By any standard of measure there are wide disparities that generally fall along racial lines.

During the retreat students should be informed of these disparities. Dialogue should be encouraged to examine minority groups historical experiences and how that might contribute to their "world view". The historical overviews that follow are included to help spur that discussion. It is recommended that handouts be made of these overviews so students can read and discuss. Discussion questions are also included to help guide the discussion.

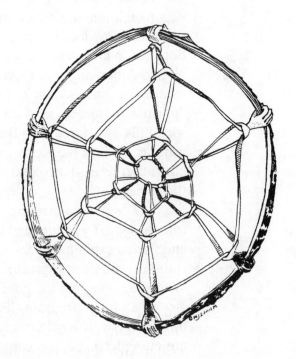

**African American
Historical Overview**

Of all American ethnic groups, African Americans have carried the heaviest burden of prejudice and discrimination (Thernstrom, 1980). Before Blacks arrived in this country in chains, there is clear evidence that Europeans viewed Africa and its inhabitants, not as the harbinger of civilization, but as beasts of burden who were less than human. Africa was usually pictured as the home of the most unmitigated form of "savagery" involving cannibalism, sexual promiscuity and strange forms of pagan ritual (ibid, 1980). Black skin was not viewed as equivalent to any other skin pigmentation but rather viewed as evil and unclean. The European psyche failed to equate blackness with beauty. Such an anti-black attitude helps explain how Europeans justified the African slave trade that lasted over three hundred years.

The racial prejudice that African Americans have been subjected to has only been a major phenomenon in the modern world. It was a direct outcome of the need to justify the slave trade. The ancient world did accept slavery as a way of life, but the ancients did not make color the focus of irrational sentiment. Nothing comparable to the violent racial prejudice of modern times existed in the ancient world. As was noted, it was not until the slave trade that skin color became the basis for discrimination. This close identification of slavery with black skin encouraged the racist idea of white supremacy.

How could the selling of human beings last for three hundred years is a question often asked. The logical explanation was there was so much money involved that countries found entire economies could be funded on slavery. Most of the countries of Europe got together and literally divided up Africa among themselves. It has been predicted that over fifty million Africans died or were sold off to slavery during this period.

Although the first Blacks to arrive on American shores were not slaves, those who came after 1619 increasingly were. As their numbers grew, so did anti-Black legislation until most slave states had laws which required blacks to be slaves for life without any rights, whites had to respect. African Americans worked from "can't see" in the morning until "can't see" at night literally fueling the American economy. Some of the most inhumane torture known to human kind was administered to the slave population to make them stand in fear. Despite their condition, Blacks contributed to the society. When Paul Revere rode through the countryside waking up people, he woke up Black minutemen as well. When George Washington crossed the Delaware river, Blacks

African American Historical Overview

were in the boat with him. Blacks have fought and died in all of America's wars. Yet when the Declaration of Independence was signed, Blacks were not included. The constitution counted African Americans as worth only three fifths of a white person's life. "Free Blacks" who escaped slavery were only slightly better off that their black bondsmen. They could not vote or hold office in southern states and were subjected to kidnapping and enslavement at any given moment.

By the 18th century slavery was institutionalized in America. Laws against interracial marriage were in place, and caste legislation produced rigid barriers between Blacks and Whites. During the revolutionary war, there were weak calls for Black manumission and ill conceived schemes for colonizing Blacks in Africa. It was not until the 1830s that the abolitionists spearheaded the first serious assault against slavery and the caste system. Defenders of the slave system responded with arguments about Black innate inferiority. Scientific, religious and political arguments were used to buttress their case.

On the eve of the Civil War, Chief Justice Taney in the Dred Scott decision of 1857 proclaimed that African Americans had no rights that Whites were bound to respect. After the Civil War and the passage of the 13th, 14th and 15th Amendments, slavery was abolished and Blacks were granted rights that Whites had learned to take for granted. For a period in U.S. history, known as reconstruction, it seemed the promise of equal opportunity for all would be achieved. Blacks were elected to federal office, some acquired land, and many were educated in "freedmen schools". Defeated white southerners however, resisted the reconstruction era with great energy. A reign of terror culminating with the emergence of the Klu Klux Klan (along with political and economic sanctions) doomed the reconstruction. When northern troops were withdrawn from the south, segregation and disfranchisement of Blacks became the rule. A series of "Jim Crow laws" legalized segregation in the South and this practice of "separate but equal" was upheld by the Supreme Court in Plessy vs Ferguson in 1896. This system of segregation remained entrenched until 1954 when the Supreme Court overturned it in Brown vs Topeka.

Less than thirty years ago the modern civil rights era began and a number of civil rights laws have been passed. While blacks have made both political and economic gains, they continue to be the most segregated group in the society, have the highest incidence of unemployment and remain victims of racial prejudice.

**Asian American
Historical Overview**

Asians represent the latest arrival of the four minority groups featured in this overview, having immigrated in substantial numbers a little over a century ago.

Unlike Blacks who were forced to come to American shores, Asians, especially the Chinese, were often invited by white land, mining and railroad barons. Although their labor contributed to the completion of the transcontinental railroad and ore mining, they encountered brutal hostility from white workers who felt the Chinese immigrants undermined their living wages by working for extremely low wages. The Chinese lifestyle which often included opium smoking was used against them by white racists as evidence that Asian culture was alien to American traditions. Opposition to Chinese immigrants was rooted in economics and racism (Reimers, 1985). Nativists claimed Chinese immigrants were unassimilable because of their race. Chinese miners found themselves faced with a foreign miners tax. In 1870 an anti-Chinese convention urged an end to Chinese immigration and the state of California passed ordinances harassing Chinese. By the 1880s anti-Chinese sentiment was so strong it led to mob violence in many western cities. One of the worst episodes occurred in Rock Springs, Wyoming in 1885. A white mob drove Chinese workers out of town, burned their homes and left twenty-eight dead (ibid, 1985).

In 1882 the Chinese Exclusion Act was passed. The Chinese became the first and only nationality to be barred by name. Immigration from China was virtually banned until the twentieth century. The racist attitudes directed at the Chinese were easily transferred to other Asian immigrants when they came to America.

Japan opened its doors to the west in 1854 but the Japanese did not immigrate in large numbers until after 1880. They soon felt the wrath of Whites who described their presence as the "yellow peril". Despite the annexation of Hawaii in 1898 which brought many Asians under U.S. Control, the hostility towards Asians increased. The San Francisco school board segregated Japanese students and in 1913 California passed a state law prohibiting Japanese from owning farm land.

Asian immigrants from Korea, India, Filipinos and other countries emigrated in smaller numbers than either Chinese or Japanese but they faced opposition to their presence similar to these groups. In 1924 Congress enacted the Oriental Exclusion Act that essentially banned all immigration from Asia. The

**Asian American
Historical Overview**

Filipinos were exempt from this Act because of the special political status of the Philippine island.

The racial hostility faced by Asians caused many to form separate communities. Today many large American cities have a "China town". During World War II anti-Asian prejudice reached its zenith when over 100,000 Japanese were interned in concentration camps.

During the contemporary period most restrictions against Asian immigration have been lifted. Wars with Asian countries have resulted in increased immigration from countries including the Philippines, Korea, Vietnam and other Southeast Asian nations.

Asians have made notable educational and economic advances in the society. Often referred to as the "model" minority (a term many reject and find offensive), their success has been used against them as they have been subjected to unwritten quotas and excluded from special initiatives designed to benefit minority groups in the society.

Hispanic American Overview

The term Hispanic encompasses a number of ethnic groups including Mexican American/Chicano, Cubans, Puerto Ricans, and other Latinos. Although each share some common ancestral ties, each possesses its own unique culture and history. This overview covers Puerto Ricans, Cubans and the largest Hispanic group-Chicanos (Mexican Americans).

Cubans

Most of the history of Cuba has been characterized by foreign domination. Columbus explored Cuba in 1492, but Spain did not colonize it until 1511. It was ruled by Spain from 1511 to 1898 (Boswell and Curtis, 1984). There were several hundred thousand Indians on the islands when the Spaniards arrived but most were extinct by the end of the 16th century as a result of massacres, disease and slavery.

Cuba served essentially as a supply and communications center between Spain and its colonies in the new world. Sugar cane, tobacco, and beef were Cuba's leading exports. The implementation of slave labor led to a large scale importation of African slaves. Like oppressed people anywhere, after years of oppressive Spanish rule, nativists rebelled. The most successful rebellion occurred in the late 1890s. This rebellion led to Cuba's fight for independence. The U.S. intervened in this war when its battleship was blown up in the Havana harbor. It declared war against Spain and the Spanish-American war that followed lasted less than four months and ended with an American victory.

Many Cubans felt the U.S. intervened only when it knew Cuba was winning its fight against Spain and also to colonize Cuba. The U.S. immediately imposed a military dictatorship on the island that lasted from 1898 to 1902. Having fought for their independence against Spain, Cubans did not want to be ruled by the Americans either and negotiated its independence from the U.S. in 1902. As a condition of its independence, America forced Cuba to accept provisions included in the Platt Amendment. This amendment allowed the U.S. to intervene in Cuban affairs and forced Cuba to provide land for a military base. The Platt Amendment was abrogated in 1934 but the U.S. still occupies a naval base on Cuba's southeastern coast (Ibid, 1984, p.17).

Much corruption characterized Cuban political life between 1902 and 1959 culminating in an intolerable situation under the dictatorship of Fulgencio Batista. Fidel Castro led the fight to overthrow Batista. After two years of fighting, Castro forced Batista to flee. Castro entered Havana triumphantly on

Hispanic American Historical Overview

January 8, 1959. Shortly afterwards, he announced that Cuba would be a socialist state. Many Cubans fled Cuba and came to America after Castro's ascension to power. Many were professional, business persons, and "white collars" who had personally benefitted under Batista's dictatorship. Immigration to the U.S. continued sporadically depending on government policy until 1980. It was the 1980 exodus however that angered many Americans. It was then that the "Mariel boat lift" was launched. Castro permitted any Cuban who wanted to leave for the U.S. to do so and over 120,000 chose to do so, departing from the Mariel harbor. This immigrant population included a criminal element. Most however were simply Cuba's poor.

Many were housed in army camps, tents and similar arrangements. While many were dispersed throughout the country, it is believed that most settled in Florida. Since the Cuban revolution, the number of Cubans living in the U.S. has grown from around 40,000 to nearly a million, (Boswell and Curtis, 1984). No other country has contributed more refugees seeking exile in the U.S. and only Mexico has contributed a greater number of emigrants to this country.

Today Cubans constitute the third largest Hispanic group ranking behind Puerto Ricans and Chicanos. The Cuban settlement is concentrated in Florida with Miami often referred to as "Little Havana". Cubans are the wealthiest of all Hispanics and have managed to preserve many of their cultural institutions intact in Miami. Cubans are also the most politically conservative, many remaining strongly anti-Castro. Cubans from the Mariel boat lift face the greatest difficulty in the society. However Cubans exercise a good deal of political, economical and social influence in Florida.

Puerto Ricans

Puerto Rico, too has a long history of foreign domination. Spain settled there in 1508. Ponce de Leon was appointed its first governor before he left to search for the "Fountain of Youth" in Florida. Like Cuba, the U.S. obtained Puerto Rico as a result of the 1898 Spanish American war. In 1900 Puerto Rico was granted legal status as a U.S. territory. In 1917 the Jones Act gave Puerto Ricans U.S. citizenship, while also making them eligible for the draft. Since the end of World War II almost one third of the population have come to America. However many have returned to the island. Still others travel back and forth, frequently

Hispanic American Historical Overview

referred to as America's first "airborne immigrants". New York and Chicago are home to the largest Puerto Rican communities in the United States.

After years of political mobilization, Puerto Ricans were permitted to elect their own governor. Luis Munoz was the first governor elected by the people. He served his country for two decades in this position. The explosive political question whether Puerto Rico should become independent or the 51st state was put on hold. In 1952 Puerto Rico was made a "Commonwealth" by an act of Congress. Puerto Rico now could raise its own flag and sing its own national anthem. It is debateable whether Commonwealth status has benefitted the U.S. or Puerto Rico more. Puerto Ricans today remain sharply divided over the questions of statehood vs independence. This issue probably won't be resolved until there is a clear consensus among the populace. Until then, the main concern is over the future of its economy. Its dependency on U.S. funding hurt the island during the Reagan administration when federal expenditures were reduced.

Puerto Rico's population continues to grow. Problems of education, unemployment, housing, and similar social ills plague the country. Puerto Ricans on the U.S. mainland face discrimination and segregation. Many fare worse economically than other Hispanic groups.

The vast majority of Puerto Ricans living in the U.S. have lived here for less than 15 years and almost half are under twenty one years of age. Puerto Ricans symbolize the basic problems of the big city. Therefore rather than viewing the problems of its Puerto Rican population as reflecting the problems of this country's urban centers, Puerto Ricans are themselves viewed as presenting a problem to the cities (Wagenheim and Wagenheim, 1973).

The Puerto Rican is often regarded as a foreigner. Puerto Ricans like most Hispanic groups are not a race, they are an ethnic group with some members white, black, and mixed (Ibid, 1973). Poverty and prejudice have made it difficult for many Puerto Ricans to progress in America.

Hispanic American Historical Overview

Chicanos

When the Spaniards arrived in the new world they found Indians like the Mayan and Aztecs who had developed high levels of civilization. The Aztecs were also known as the Mexicas and from this term the country eventually was named Mexico (Meier and Rivera, 1972). In 1502 Emperor Montezuma II rose to lead the Aztec empire. Tenochtitlan (Mexico City, today) was the capital and when the Spaniards entered in 1519 they were astounded at the extensive markets featuring a variety of produce (Ibid, 1972 p.9).

In 1519 the Spanish conquistador Herman Cortes with over 500 men landed on the gulf coast of Mexico and in less than three years had imposed Spanish rule on the Aztec empire. After Conquering the Aztecs, the Spaniards eventually took control of all Mexico, Central America and the southwestern part of the U.S. The Spaniards could not have been successful in their conquest without the aid of friendly Indian nation states.

Wherever they conquered, the Spaniards imposed the Catholic religion and their culture. The Spaniards brought relatively few Spanish women so there was much intermingling. This fusion of Indian and Spanish produced the"mestizo".

In the 1500s Spanish explorers ventured as far as Florida in the southeast. There were Spanish settlements in California and Arizona years before the English settled Jamestown. Near the close of the 18th century the western world was caught up in revolutionary fervor. The U.S. revolution was soon followed by the French revolution and two decades later, the Mexican revolution occurred. Between Mexican independence in 1821 and its war with the U.S. in 1846, there was considerable migration to what is now the southwest U.S. (Ibid, 1972 p.33).

Early in the 19th century Americans began to embrace "manifest destiny"-the chosen race theory (Ibid, 1972 p. 56). Americans believed they were destined to control land from the Atlantic to the Pacific ocean. In 1836 Texas declared its independence from Mexico and in 1845 was annexed by the U.S. an event that Mexico warned would lead to war. In 1846 war erupted between Mexico and the U.S. Mexico was defeated and in 1848 signed the treaty of Guadalupe Hidalgo. Through this treaty the U.S. acquired Arizona,California, Nevada, New Mexico, Utah, half of Colorado and received clear title to Texas. Mexicans living in the ceded area were given a year to decide whether to become U.S. citizens or not. Although they were promised they would maintain ownership of their land, they soon found the land gone,

Hispanic American Historical Overview

Chicanos

their religious beliefs questioned and themselves victims of increasing hostile laws and customs. The American take over of the southwest was much more than a military and political victory; it also initiated Anglo penetration of the economy and eventual control of the entire society (Mirande, 1985). From 1848 to the end of the nineteenth century, Anglos migrated to the southwest resulting in Mexican Americans ending up in a Minority position in what had been their own land (Mier and Rivera, 1972).

The discovery of gold in California and the gold rushes that followed in 1849 brought a massive influx of Anglos to that region. The highly competitive gold rush led to massive discrimination against Mexican Americans whom many Anglo vigilante groups tried to ban from the gold mines.

The treaty of Guadalupe Hidalgo separated the two countries politically but not culturally. Mexicans crossed the border both ways frequently. As economic conditions worsened in Mexico, migration increased. The first significant wave came in the early 1900s; the second and much larger wave lasted through the 1920s. The third wave came after WWII. Mexican immigrant laborers were used extensively in agriculture but they also helped on the railroads and during war time in major factories throughout the U.S. They had few rights and when their services were no longer needed, many were departed. The increased Mexican immigration faced its greatest opposition during periods of recession in the U.S. economy. Whenever jobs were scare U.S. workers demanded action restricting Mexican immigration. Usually powerful agricultural lobbyists were successful in maintaining an "open border" for Mexican laborers however.

The Mexican population continues to grow today and is the fastest growing population in the U.S. Chicanos have made the U.S. the fourth largest Spanish speaking country in the world. They face a Minority status in the society which translates into inferior schooling, high unemployment, greater health risks and similar social and economic discrepancies faced by Blacks.

Native American Historical Overview

Bury My Heart at Wounded Knee by Dee Brown offers a powerful accounting of the conquest of the American West from a Native American perspective. It describes in heartbreaking detail the massacres and horifying atrocities perpetrated against Native Americans to gain the land.

"They made us many promises, more than I can remember, but they never kept but one; they promised to take our land, and they took it" (Brown, 1971).

The above quote by an anonymous Indian typifies their contact with the "white man". When Columbus ended up on the shores of the new world, he named the people who welcomed him "Indios". Columbus was so favorably taken by the way he was treated that he wrote to the King and Queen of Spain the following:

"So tractable, so peaceable are these people, that I swear to your Majesties there is not in the world a better nation. They love their neighbors as themselves and their discourse is ever sweet and gentle, and accompanied with a smile; and though it is true they are naked, yet their manners are decorous and praiseworthy" (Brown, 1971).

Despite Columbus's initial praise, Europeans viewed such attributes as signs of weakness and savagery. Most early accounts of European explorers described Native Americans as behaving like wild animals and questioned their humanity. As a result there was a constant dichotomy at play between Europeans who felt Indians could be "civilized" and those who proposed at best apartheid conditions for Native Americans and at worse genocide.

Early European settlements in the 1600s undertook missionary work and attempted to convert and "civilize" Native Americans. This process of "civilization" required Indians to divest themselves of everything that made them Indian in order to be assimilated. This price tag of cultural suicide became too great for many, so resistance escalated in the form of Indian rebellions. As more and more European settlers began to displace natives and take their land, more and more natives began to resist, resulting in the "Indian" wars. When war began, assimilationists took a back seat to those bent on conquest. The policy of assigning Native Americans to reservations resulted from the "Indian" wars, although many were enslaved.

Later when America gained its independence, government sanctioned removal of Native Americans westward, occurred on a massive scale. The period between 1780 and the 1840s witnessed

**Native American
Historical Overview**

the removal of numerous tribes including the south's "five civilized tribes". One of the platforms that helped elect Andrew Jackson to the Presidency was his promise to remove Native Americans from the southeast. Jackson carried out this promise and although Congress passed an Act designating much of the land west of the Mississippi river "Native American land", this like every other treaty was broken. When the war with Mexico ended, Native American land became "white man's" land. It was also during this period that the concept of manifest destiny became the de facto policy. It was widely touted that Europeans were ordained by their God to dominate all of America. Territory acquired through conquest and invasion now became states.

After the civil war the Dawes Act of 1887 represented the new Native American policy (Thernstrom, 1980). This Act permitted the division of communally held tribal lands into individual allotments. The allotment period lasting into the 1930's resulted in massive loss of Native American land. Federal agents wielded enormous power on the reservations and tribal governments benefitted little from Bureau of Indian Affairs policies. When Congress extended U.S. citizenship rights to Native Americans in 1924, questions of Native American treaty rights remain unsettled. In 1934 the Indian Reorganization Act ended the allotment program and tribes could once again own land communally.

Today Native Americans struggle to maintain sovereign rights that are supposed to be protected by treaties. Politically, economically and educationally, Native Americans remain one of the most disadvantaged groups in the society.

Overview Discussion Questions

These questions can be used to stimulate discussion on the historical overviews:

1. What do Minority groups in the society have in common?

2. Does America owe Minorities anything, other than an equal opportunity?

3. Should Minorities receive reparations or some form of financial payment to atone for their treatment in the society?

4. Do you think each Minority group faces racial prejudice today?

5. Is racism a major strand throughout U.S. history?

6. Is America basically a racist nation?

7. What do you think are the reasons for present day problems of race?

8. Do you think America's racial problems will ever be resolved?

9. Would you say Minorities face more class discrimination than racial discrimination?

10. What should be done to improve the economic status of Minorities in the country?

Overview Bibliography

Boswell, Thomas D. ; Curtis, James R. (1984). *The Cuban-American Experience Culture, Images and Perspectives*. Rawman & Allanheld Publishers, Totowa, New Jersey.

Brown, Dee A. (1970). *Bury My Heart at Wounded Knee*. New York: Holt, Rinehart, and Winston.

Carrion, Arturo M. (1983). *Puerto Rico A Political and Cultural History*. W.W. Norton & Company Inc. New York.

Meier, Matts, Rivera, Feliciano (Eds) (1974). *Readings on La Raza The Twentieth Century*. Hill and Wang. New York.

Mirande, Alfredo (1985). *The Chicano Experience, An Alternative Perspective*, University of Notre Dame Press, Notre Dame, IN.

Reimers, David M. (1985). *Still the Golden Door-The Third World Comes to America*. Columbia University Press, New York.

Thernstrom, Stephen (Ed) (1980). *Harvard Encyclopedia of American Ethnic Groups*, Harvard University Press, Cambridge, MA.

Wagenheim, Kal; Wagenheim, Olga Jimenes de (1973). *A Documentary History, The Puerto Ricans*. Praeger Publishers. New York.

Weyer, Thomas (1988). *Hispanic USA-Breaking The Melting Pot*. Harper & Row Publishers. New York.

Immigrants-the newest Minorities?

Historical experience in the U.S. has demonstrated that assignments of immigrant groups to low status positions in the opportunity structure have often been made primarily upon the basis of race (Spencer, 1988). While waves of white ethnics from Europe brought different languages and cultural experiences, after one or two generations they were allowed to "melt" into the society. Skin color has prevented other immigrants from enjoying the same privileges. This poses serious problems for the future because the vast majority of those currently immigrating to the U.S. are non-white people from Latin America, the Caribbean and Asia (Cockcroft 1986, cited in Spencer, 1988).

Between 1983 and 1986, Mexican born immigrants made up the largest share of legal immigrants to the U.S., about 60,000 a year. The Philippines contributed about 46,000 and immigrants form Korea and Vietnam average nearly 35,000 each. A host of other third world countries contribute thousands each year as well (Allen and Turner, 1988).

Both Asian and Mexican immigrant populations rose dramatically during the 80s. A small but growing proportion of immigrants are coming from Central America and Africa, while the share coming from predominantly white European countries has declined from 53% in the 1950s to less than 12% today (Ibid,1988).

Nearly 90 percent of recent immigrants live in metropolitan areas where most of America's racial Minorities live. As a result many immigrants are currently labeled as Minorities, suffering a similar status to other people of color. Mexican and Haitian immigrants, for example, share a status similar to Blacks.
This status is sometimes less severe based on the reasons immigrants are in America. As a result some are more welcome than others. The Vietnamese were seen as more deserving than the Cubans from the Mariel boatlift. Koreans may come to carry a positive racial stereotype, where as Mexicans may come to be stigmatized (Matthews, 1985 cited in Spencer, 1988).

Although most still come to better their economic conditions, many immigrants arrive in the U.S. to escape war and oppression. Their arrival in such large numbers poses serious problems for the society. Many are perceived as taking away American jobs. They require a myriad of human services. Their presence has resulted in tensions among Minority groups who are forced to share scare resources.

Should immigrants of color be viewed as racial Minorities? Discuss.

Notes

Allen, James P.,Turner, Eugene J. (1988). *"Immigrants", American Demographics*. September.

Archdeacon, Thomas J. (1983). *Becoming American, An Ethnic History*. The Free Press. New York, NY.

Coppa, Frank J., Curran, Thomas J. (1976). *The Immigrant Experience in America*. Twayne Publishers. Boston.

Reimers, David M. (1985). *Still the Golden Door-The Third World Comes to America*. Columbia University Press. New York.

Spencer, David. (May, 1988). *Transitional Bilingual Education and the Socialization of Immigrants*. Harvard Educational Review, Vol 58 No 2.

Resource

Center for Migration Studies (CMS)
209 Flags Place
Staten Island, NY 10304-1199
(718) 351-8800
 CMS is an educational, nonprofit institute founded in New York in 1964, committed to encourage and facilitate the study of sociodemographic, economic, political, historical, legislative and pastoral aspects of human migration and refugee movements.

Pluralism vs the Melting Pot

"... But why can't we all be the same. I mean I don't look at skin color. I try to treat everyone the same - what's wrong with that?"

You have probably heard the above sentiment expressed on numerous occasions; perhaps not the exact words but the meaning was essentially the same. Usually the person who voices this sentiment is well intentioned and would not deliberately try to be insensitive to the cultural needs of others. Unfortunately treating everyone the same does not mean everyone is being treated fairly. Too often treating everyone the same means believing that everyone has the same needs or will respond in predictable ways.

Perhaps a simple example will help clarify why this particular sentiment needs to be challenged. In planning your retreat, if cultural preferences were not taken into consideration, what type of food would you serve? What type of music would you plan for the participants to listen to? What speakers would you invite to address the gathering? Although these examples are somewhat simplistic they do speak to the real importance of pluralism in thought and action. Pluralism depends on diversity. The melting pot thrives on conformity.

When one is expressing the sentiment of ignoring differences, one is generally supporting the melting pot theory. This theory of assimilation was popularized by Israel Zangwill (1909) in a play, *The Melting Pot*.

During the 1800s the U.S. was host to a wave of immigrants from Europe. As the number of immigrants from southern Eastern bloc European countries increased, white Anglo-Saxon protestants began to feel their values and life styles were threatened. As a result immigration laws were changed. These changes proved discriminatory to "dark skinned" Europeans as well as to people of color the world over.

Since thousands of immigrants had entered the country prior to the immigration laws being changed, ways had to be found to acculturate the immigrant population to U.S. society as quickly as possible. The public schools served this role probably better than any other institution, although most of the institutions of the society contributed to immigrant assimilation. Immigrants were expected to downplay their own particular ethnic heritage and traditions and replace them with new American traditions and values. Zangwill (1909) attempted to describe this transformation when he wrote:

Pluralism vs the Melting Pot

"America is God's crucible, the melting pot where all the races of Europe are melting and reforming!"

The idea of a distinct entity - an "American" was being widely pushed until it was firmly established by the beginning of the twentieth century. Now, when immigrants wanted to maintain their language or customs they were accused of being un-American.

Although Europeans were encouraged to melt, generally people of color were not permitted to. It is not surprising that the melting pot concept is rejected by many people of color today. Cultural pluralism is the concept being embraced by such groups. Gold (1977) offers a reason for this when he writes.

". . . Multiculturalism equates with the respect shown the varied cultures and ethnic groups which have built the United States and which continue today to contribute to its richness and diversity."

Multiculturalism recognizes that as Americans we share many things in common but as hyphenated Americans our life styles and values need not be the same. The way we dance, speak, party, dress, etc. can reflect our cultural heritage and need not be considered anti-American. Multiculturalism attempts to make the point that differences are not deficiencies.

The melting pot theory essentially says, "from the many, one", while the pluralism theory says, "the one is really many".

It is important that these two concepts be discussed during the retreat. Helping students accept differences is more than just teaching toleration. Practicing diversity is key to our survival as a nation and as a member of the world community.

It does not take much effort to understand the implications of expecting everyone to be "like us". Nations spend billions of dollars on weapons systems because other nations are communist or Moslem. We need to help students understand that treating everyone the same has resulted in the inadequate treatment and exclusion of the contributions made by minorities in text books, underrepresentation of minorities on school staffs and lack of authentic involvement of minorities in the decision making structures of the society.

Notes

Gold, Milton J. (1977). "Pressure Points in Multicultural Education" in *In Praise of Diversity: A Resource Book for Multicultural Education*, (eds) Gold, Grant and Rivlin, Washington, DC: Teacher Corps: Association of Teacher Educators.

Zangwill, Israel (1909). *The Melting Pot*, New York: MacMillan and Company

Colangelo, Nicholas, et al. (1979). *Multicultural Non-Sexist Education*, Kenda II/Hunt Publishing Company.

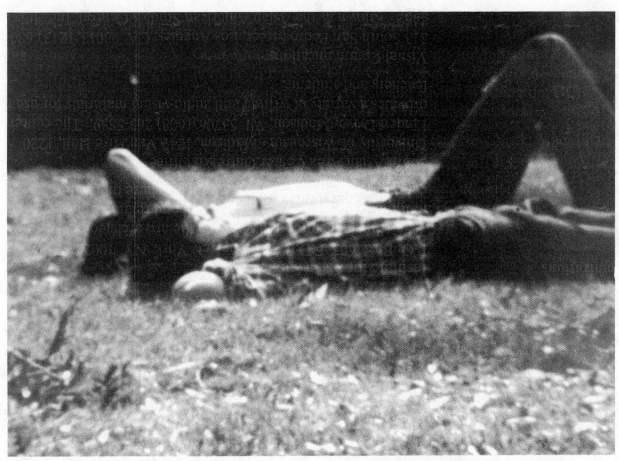

During the retreat, there was time just to relax and reflect

Tips For Working With Culturally Different Students

Working with culturally different students is a challenge that requires sensitivity and vulnerability. Because of the potential for mixed signals, suspicion and misunderstanding it's important that care be given to how this interaction is to be structured. While do's and don'ts are unnecessary it is important to acknowledge some broad generalizations that may prove helpful when working with racial minorities. If these guidelines are followed you stand a better chance of creating positive interactions.

* Avoid the tendency to lump all minorities together or view them as the same.

* Stress cultural pluralism and celebrate diversity while discarding the notion of the U.S. as a melting pot.

* Watch for stereotyping in language, roles, media and in institutional practices.

* Recognize that by treating everyone the "same" does not mean that everyone is being treated fairly.

* Become familiar with different historical world views that each minority group represents. Although George Washington might be considered an American hero to whites, since he owned slaves he may be considered just the opposite by blacks.

* Develop a contemporary perspective about race and culture. Read minority publications and listen to it's leadership.

* Be more accepting of minority descriptions and perceptions of their life experiences in America.

* Take some risks. Attend activities and events that are sponsored by individuals outside your ethnic group.

* Participate in workshops, conferences and classes that deal with race and culture.

* Involve minorities in the planning of programs.

CHAPTER 3

African American Resources

Books

Bennett, Lerone, Jr. *Before the Mayflower: A history of the Negro in America:1619-1964.* Baltimore: Penguin Books,1967.

Davis, Y. Angela, (ed.) *If They Come in the Morning: Voices of Resistance.* New York: New American Library, 1971.

Franklin, John Hope. *From Slavery to Freedom: A History of Black Americans.* 4th ed. New York: Knopf, 1974.

Marable, Manning, *How Capitalism Underdeveloped Black America: Problems in Race, Political Economy and Society,* Boston: South End Press, 1983.

Staples, Robert, (ed.) *The Black Family: Essays and Studies,* Revised Edition, Belmont, California: Wadsworth Publishing Company,1982.

Afro-American Publishing, Inc.
910 South Michigan, Suite 556
Chicago, IL 60605 Tel: 312/922-1147
Eugene Winslow, President; Loretta Rivers, Business Manager. A mail order operation specializing in black/integrated educational materials selected for building racial pride and interracial understanding including toys, games, pictures, records, books, paperbacks, and filmstrips. Free catalog available on request.

The Black Resource Guide
A National Black Directory. This book lists over 3,000 nationally known black organizations, institutions, businesses, and public figures. To order your copy, contact: Black Resource Guide, 501 Oneida Place NW, Washington, DC 20011, (202) 291-4373.

Organization

ASALH
The Association for the Study of Afro-American Life and History, Inc., Dept E, 1401 14th Street NW, Washington, DC 20005, (202) 667-2822. Publishes excellent Black History kits and also determines the theme for Black History week annually.

Films

Black American Cinema Society
c/o Western States Black Research Center
3617 Montclair Street
Los Angeles, CA 90018 Tel: 213/737-3292
Has black film collection.

Films

"Of Black America Series: Black History: Lost, Stolen or Strayed"
BFA Educational Media, Santa Monica, CA
A revealing film about Black-White relations in America narrated by Bill Cosby.

Videos

Blacast Productions
199-19 Linden Blvd.
St. Albans, NY 11434 (718) 527-2417
Provides quality Black videos, entertainment, and lectures.

"The Black Contribution: Where You There? Series"
Beacon Films
P.O. Box 575
Norwood, MA 02062
This series focuses on the contributions Blacks have made to the U.S. in the twentieth century. Also available in viedo.

"Our Time Has Come: Jesse Jackson"
Social Studies School Service
Culver City, CA
A video of Jesse Jackson's speech at the 1984 Democratic National Convention. This speech can serve as a springboard for a discussion of Black participation in U.S. politics.

"The Second American Revolution"
PBS Video
1320 Braddock Place
Alexandria, VA 22314
115-minute two-part presentation, Ossie Davis, Ruby Dee and Bill Moyers discuss the achievements of African Americans.

Asian American Resources

Books

Asian American Materials
c/o JACP, Inc.
414 East Third Avenue
San Mateo, CA 94401 Tel: 415/343-9408
Retail outlet for Asian American Materials; $2 for catalog.

Cheng-Tsu Wu, Ed. *Chink! A Documentary History of Anti-Chinese Prejudice in America.* New York: World Publishing, 1972.

Daniels, Roger. *Asian America: Chinese and Japanese in the United States Since 1850.* (1988) University of Washington Press.

Hosokawa, William K. *Nisei: The Quiet American.* New York, 1969.

Kim, Hyung-Chan, (ed.) *Dictionary of Asian American History.* 1986 67.95. Greenwood Press.

Kitano, Harry H. and Daniels, Roger. *Asian Americans: The Emerging Minority.* 1988 .

Okihiro, Gary Y. et al., (eds.) *Reflections on Shattered Windows: Promises and Prospects for Asian American Studies.* 1988. Washington State University Press.

Weglyn, Michi. *Years of Infamy: The Untold Story of America's Concentration Camps.* New York: William Morrow, 1976.

Organizations

The Asia Society
The Asia Society is a non-profit, non-political, public education organization dedicated to increasing American understanding of Asia and its growing importance to U.S. and world relations. It publishes a research journal for educators, professionals, and those interested in Asia. The journal *Focus on Asian Studies* includes feature articles, essays on the arts and literature, book reviews, perspectives on Asia by Asians, model curricula, resource listings and a calendar of major Asia related events across the country. Subscription is $5.00 per year from Focus on Asian Studies, P.O. Box 1308-M, Fort Lee, NJ 07024. Offices for the Asia Society are located at 725 Park Avenue, New York, NY 10021.

Chinese Culture Foundation
750 Kearny Street, San Francisco, CA 94108, (415) 986-1822. The Foundation publishes historical, cultural arts and educational material.

Organizations

Institute for Asian Studies, Inc.
P.O. Box 1603, F.D.R. Station, New York, NY 10022, (212) 535-7496. Single lectures and series on the art, archaeology, history, literature, philosophy, religion, travel and related aspects of Asian culture for the adult audience. Free brochure on request.

South Asian Area Center Outreach Office
University of Wisconsin - Madison, 1249 Van Hise Hall, 1220 Linden Drive, Madison, WI 53706, (608) 263-5839. The center provides a variety of written and audio-visual materials for use by teachers and students.

Visual Communications
313 South San Pedro Street, Los Angeles, CA 90013, (213) 680-4462. Known as the Asian American Studies Central, Inc., it is a media organization that produces material on the experiences of Asian Americans.

Films

Asian Cinevision, Inc.
32 East Broadway
New York, NY 10002
Send for Catalog

"Becoming Americans"
Kev Levine
Irish Films
720 West Blaine
Seattle, WA 98119
This one hour documentary focuses on the Hmong refugees from Laos.

East Asia Resource Center
University Washington (DR-05)
Seattle, WA 98195   Tel: 206/543-1921
Films on China, Japan and Korea

"Guilty by Reason of Race"
NBC Educational Enterprises, New York
TV documentary film about the problems of Japanese Americans during and after World War II.

Videos

Asian Cinevision
32 E. Broadway
New York, NY 10002 (212) 925-8685

"Unfinished Business: The Japanese American Internment
Cases"
JACP, Inc.
414 East Third Avenue
San Mateo, CA 94401
This hour-long documentary tells of three Japanese Americans
who refused to be interned, their conviction, and their legal battle
to overturn their convictions. Available as a 16mm film, Beta or
VHS.

"Japanese Relocation"
Social Studies School Service
Culver City, CA
This video tells the story of the internment of Japanese Americans
during World War II. (Beta or VHS)

"The Way of the Willow"
Beacon Films
Norwood, MA
A thirty minute video which presents a story that describes the
problems faced by a Vietnamese immigrant family when it first
settles in a North American community.

Hispanic American Resources

Books

Acuna, Rodolfo. Occupied America: *The Chicano's Struggle Toward Liberation*. Canfield, Harper and Row, 1980.

Castro, Tony. *Chicano Power*. E.P. Dutton & Co. Saturday Review Press, 1974.

Gonzales, Rodolfo. *I Am Joaquin*. Bantam, 1972.

Lazo, Mario. *Dagger in the Heart!* New York: Twain Circle Publishing Company, 1968.

Wagneheim, Kal, with de Wagenheim, Olga Jiminez,(eds.). *The Puerto Ricans: a documentary History*. Garden City: Doubleday, 1973.

Organizations

Center for Puerto Rican Studies
Hunter College, 695 Park Avenue, New York, NY 10021, (212) 772-5689. A research unit that promotes an integral analysis of Puerto Rican society, establishing links between the island situation and its extensions in the barrios of the United States.

National Association for Bilingual Education (NABE)
1201 16th Street NW, Rm 407, Washington, DC 20036, (202) 822-7870. Contact Person: Dr. Gene T. Chavez, Center for Multicultural Outreach, 7401 Metcalf Ave., Overland Park, KS 66204, (913) 722-0272. NABE's clientele consists of educators, parents, and others interested in bilingual education. Nation wide it has thirtytwo state affiliates. It sponsors an annual conference and provides general information on bilingual information. It publishes the *NABE Journal* and *NABE News*. Costs for membership depend on the category for the new member and length for desired membership. Individual membership in NABE includes a subscription to the *NABE Journal* as well as *NABE News*.

Films

Chicano Film Guide
University of Texas - Austin
c/o Publications - The General Libraries
P.O. Box P
Austin, TX 78912   Guide Costs $5

"I am Joaquin"
El Teatro Campesino, San Juan Bautisa, CA
The epic poem of the Chicano movement is dramatised in this film.

Resources For Your Retreat

Films

Icarus Films
Icarus Films have a large and comprehensive collection of films and videotapes on Central America, the Caribbean and South America. They have several new releases, some of which have been nominated for and received international awards. They are entitled "Banana Company, Americans In Transition", an invaluable exploration of the background to the upheaval in Central America today; "Dawn of the People", the Nicaraguan literacy crusade of 1980; "Decision to Win", life and aims of the FMLN guerrilla army in El Salvador; "Golden Dove First", prizewinner at the Leipzig International Film Festival and finally for lovers of Latin American music, "The Central American Peace Concert" is a stunning videotape of 150 renowned singers and musicians from all over Latin America, who came together in Managua to entertain and encourage a crowd of 50,000 with songs of peace, as Ex-Somosa guardsman attacked Nicaragua from bases in Honduras. For a complete list and further information contact: Icarus Films, 200 Park Avenue South, Suite 1319, New York, NY 10003.

"Island is America"
Anti-Defamation League of B'nai B'rith
823 United Nations Plaza
New York, NY 10017
Depicts the cultural, social and economic life of mainland Puerto Ricans.

Music

Cris Plata
1220 Lois Dr.
Sun Prairie, WI 53590
(608) 837-9451
Cris is a singer-songwriter from San Antonio, Texas. His Mexican-American heritage and Texan background influence his strong rhythms and lyrics. His music has been described as an energetic mix of Tex-Mex and country folk music. Cris can be booked as a solo act or with his talented band. For booking reach Cris at the above address. Also available is his newly released album "Spreading the Rumor".

Native American Resources

Books

Baird, David W. *The Vanishing American, White Attitudes and U.S. Indian Policy*. Wesleyan University Press, 1981.

Brown, Dee A. *Bury My Heart at Wounded Knee*. New York: Holt, Rinehart, and Winston, 1970 and 1971.

Debo, Angie. *A History of the Indians of the United States*. 1986. University of Oklahoma Press.

Deloria, Vine. *Behind the Trails of Broken Treaties: An Indian Declaration of Independence*. New York: Delacorte Press, 1974.

Foreman, Grant. *Indian Removal: The Emmigration of the Five Civilized Tribes of Indians*. Norman: University of Oklahoma Press, 1982.

Gilbert, Hila. *Making Two Worlds One and the Story of All-American Indian Days*. 1986. Connections Press, WY.

Hoxie, Frederick E. *Indians in American History*. 1988. Harlan Davidson.

Iverson, Peter, (ed.) *The Plains Indians of the Twentieth Century*. 1985. University of Oklahoma Press.

Kopper, Philip. *The Smithsonian Book of North American Indians: Before the Coming of Europeans*. 1986. Smithsonian Books.

Native American Directory
Native American Directory, P.O. Box 5000, San Carlos, AZ 85550-0301. A quick reference for locating Native American Organizations, events, medias, tribal offices and reservations. Special guide for acquiring native art forms through galleries, Native American stores, and trading posts. References Alaska, Canada and the United States. Published by the National Native American Cooperative, Fred Synder, Director.

Matlock, Gary. *Enemy Ancestors: The Anasazi World, With a Guide to Sites*. 1988. Northland.

Stedman, Raymond W. *Shadows of the Indian: Stereotypes in American Culture*. 1986. University of Oklahoma Press.

Weatherford, Jack. *Indian Givers. Crown Publishers: New York., 1988.*

Resources For Your Retreat

Organizations

National Indian Institute, Inc.
Suburban Route, Box 1982, Rapid City, SD 57702, (605) 348-6138. The institute trains Native Americans in a wide range of management seminars, operates speakers programs, a newsletter, and more.

Huntington Free Library and Reading Room
9 Westchester Square, Bronx, NY 10461, (212) 829-7770
The Huntington Free Library and Reading Room is the depository library for the Museum of the American Indian. Open to the public by appointment, its extensive reference collection contains information on the archaeology, ethnology and history of the native peoples of the Americas. Works on Native American languages, current affairs, art and biography are also included. The Library is noted for its extensive collection of current and retrospective Native American newspapers, as well as a wide selection of historical and anthropological journals from North, Central and South America.

Films

"How the West Was Won . . . and Honor Lost"
McGraw-Hill Textfilms, New York.
This is a film of the betrayal of the Native Americans through broken treaties and removal.

NAPBC Program Catalog
The Native American Public Broadcasting Consortium, Inc., (NAPBC) publishes a catalog that is a compilation of available films and videos that cover Native American history, culture, education, economic development, current events and the arts. As a NAPBC library member it is possible for TV stations, schools and educational organizations to use the programs. Programs are also available on rental basis to non-members. For more information contact: NAPBC, P.O. Box 83111, Lincoln, NE 68501, (402) 472-3522.

Tapes

Woodland Indians
This series of sixty-five short radio features gives voice to the contemporary concerns, diverse heritage and rich culture unique to these Americans. Cassettes are now available at $9 per cassette of $27 for the entire series. To order contact WHA Radio, 821 University Avenue, Madison, WI 53706, (608) 263-3970. Checks payable to WHA Radio.

Video

"May Our Education Not Betray Our Traditions"
The video taped program is available from the University of Montana Native American Studies program. It features representatives from various tribes, which include the Gree, Pine Ridge, Blackfeet, and more. Copies of the tape are made available by writing to: Youthgrant Project, NAS-KYI-YO, 730 Eddy, Missoula, MT 59812, (406) 243-5831.

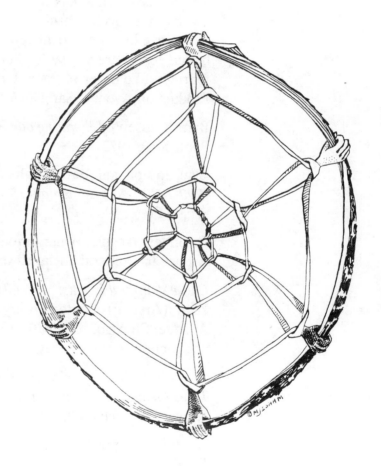

Multicultural Resources

Books

Allport, Gordon W. *The Nature of Prejudice.* Garden City, New York: Doubleday, 1958.

Anderson, Charles H. *White Protestant Americans: From National Origins to a Religious Group.* Englewood Cliffs, New Jersey: Prentice Hall, 1970.

The Annual Series: 1972 - 1985
Founding Editors: J. William Pfeiffer and John E. Jones
Current Editors: Leonard D. Goodstein and J. William Pfeiffer
These fourteen annuals contain: structured experiences that involve students in learning by doing, handouts, charts, diagrams, innovative ideas, practical applications and much more. Paperbound copies are available. Substantial discount when ordering all fourteen. To order contact: University Associates, Inc., 8517 Production Avenue, San Diego, CA 92121, (619) 578-5900.

Barndt, Joseph. *Liberating our White Ghetto.* Minnesota: Augsburg Publishing, 1972.

Blau, Joseph, and Baron, Salo, (eds.) *The Jews in the United States, 1790-1840: A Documentary History.* New York: Columbia University Press, 1963.

Campbell, Anguss. *White Attitudes Toward Black People.* Ann Arbor: Institute on Social Research Press, 1971.

Chase's Annual Events: Special days, Weeks, and Months in the Year. (Annual) Contemporary Books, Inc., 180 North Michigan Avenue, Chicago, IL 60601. Lists both official and unofficial designations of all the days of the year.

Goldstein, Sidney, and Goldschieder, Calvin. *Jewish Americans: Three Generations in a Jewish Community.* Englewood Cliffs, New Jersey: Prentice Hall, 1968.

Greeley, Andrew M. *Why Can't They Be Like Us? America's White Ethnic groups.* New York: Dutton, 1975.

Guide to Multicultural Resources
A comprehensive listing of multicultural resources can be obtained by ordering this directory (1989 edition). Send $58.00 plus 3.50 for handling to: Praxis Publications, Inc., P.O. Box 9869, Madison, WI 53715, (608) 244-5633.

Books

The Institute of Texan Cultures
Hemisfair Plaza/P.O. Box 1226, San Antonio, TX 78294, (512) 226-7651. The *Chinese Texans* is a booklet that presents a brief history of Chinese Texans with numerous photographs and a reading list. Also has other publications and audio-visuals on other Texan minority groups.

Kerner Commission. *National Advisory Commission on Civil Rights.* New York: Bantam, 1968.

Lead On ! The Complete Handbook for Group Leaders
The authors are Leslie G. Lawson, Franklyn Donant and John Lawson. This book is a comprehensive guide for leaders of volunteer groups. Twenty-four easy to follow chapters describe essentials for novices and experienced leaders. Indispensable for leaders of youth clubs, church programs, college organizations, etc. The price is $5.95 for paperback and can be ordered from: Impact Publishers, P.O. Box 1094, San Luis Obispo, CA 93406, (805) 534-5911.

Meltzer, Milton. *Never to Forget: The Jews of the Holocaust.* New York: Harper and Row, 1976.

Playfair
The authors are Matt Weinstein and Joel Goodman. This book, billed as everybody's guide to noncompetitive play is filled with games for people who are interested in learning about a new type of play that lets people be supportive, cooperative and open with each other. The price is $8.95 and can be ordered through: Impact Publishers, P.O. Box 1094, San Luis Obispo, CA 93406, (805) 543-5911.

Roommate Negotiation Workbook
Offers a step by step guide to preventing disputes and to resolving disagreements when they do arise. The workbook teaches students the same techniques used by professional negotiators and is part of a larger program aimed at teaching students practical social skills they will need throughout their lives. Contact: Dr. Barbara Engram, Hood College, Frederick, MD 21701, (301) 663-3131, ext. 229.

Books

Sproul, Barbara C. *Primal Myths: Creating The World*. 1979.
Harper and Row Publishers, Inc.
10 East 53rd Street
New York, NY 10022
Includes creation myths from every part of the globe. It is perhaps the most comprehensive collection of creation myths ever assembled. Students should be fasinated by the comparison of African, Near Eastern, European, and Native American myths that explain civilization's beginning.

Terry, R. *For Whites Only*. Grand Rapids, Michigan: Erdmans, Puritan 1970.

Thernstrom, Stephen, (ed.) *Harvard Encyclopedia of American Ethnic Groups*. The Belknap Press of Harvard University Press. Cambridge, Massachusetts and London, England, 1980.

Organizations

Anti-Defamation League of B'nai B'rith (ADL)
823 United Nations Plaza
New York, NY 10017 Tel: 212/409-1515

Council of Interracial Books for Children Racism/Sexism Resource Center
1841 Broadway
New York, NY 10023 Tel: 212/757-5339

The Multicultural Christian Education Resources Center.
Scarritt College, 1008 19th Avenue South, Nashville, TN 37203, (615) 327-2700. Director: Prof. Charles Foster. Joe Nash, Consultant, Multicultural Workshops. The Center has nation-wide potential for particular Christian education ventures and conferences. Program emphasizes workshops, seminars, retreats, TV talk shows, and consultations.

National Race Unity Committee
The National Race Unity Committee is an active committee of the National Spiritual Assembly of the Baha' is of the United States. Its mandate is to identify the trends in race relations, within and without the Baha'i community and to recommend to the National Spiritual Assembly the actions to be taken and programs to be adopted by the Baha'i community to meet the insistent challenge of racial prejudice. For additional information, contact National Race Unity Committee, c/o Washington Baha'i Center, 5713 16th Street NW, Washington, DC 20011.

Facilitator

Charles Taylor, author of this book, is available to facilitate your retreat. Write to him c/o Praxis Publications, Inc. P.O. Box 9869, Madison, WI 53715 (608) 244-5633.

Films

Modern Talking Picture Service
5000 Park Street
St. Petersburg, FL 33709
Loans films to organizations free of charge. Write for their catalog.

Publication and Films
1717 Massachusetts Ave, NW
Washington, DC 20036
Some films are free. Send for catalog.

RACE RELATIONS: A Feature and Documentary Filmography
An annotated listing of 223 films addressing race relations.
Available from the Center of Study of Human Rights,704 S.I.A., Columbia University, New York, NY 10027 Tel: 212/280-2479
Price $5. Make Check payable to Columbia University.

Videos

"A Class Divided"
PBS Video
1230 Braddock Place
Alexandria, VA 22134
This video discusses the long-range effects, twenty years, of a class experiment in which the teacher treated students differently based on eye color. See also: "The Eye of the Storm".

"A Tale of O on Being Different"
The O makes the X's a group. The X's never knew they had so much in common until the O walked into the room. They did not have to think much about being X's before, but now they are X-tra self-conscious. "A Tale of O" is an entertaining, educational program about what happens to any new or different kind of person in a group and how to manage that situation. Write Goodmeasure, Inc., P.O. Box 3004, Cambridge, MA 02139, (617) 942-2714. The video is highly recommended for Cultural Retreats.

"The Eye of the Storm"
Social Studies School Services
Culver City, CA
A 27 minute video. A teacher demonstrates to her students the effects of prejudice by separating her class into "inferior" and "superior" groups based on eye color. See Also "a Class Divided".

Resources For Your Retreat

Videos

"Racism 101"
PBS Video
1320 Braddock Place
Alexandria, VA 22314
Tel: 800/424-7963 or 703/739-5380
This program in the award winning Frontline series, takes you to campuses that have been marred by racial unrest in recent years and explains why the confrontations continue.
Purchase in VHS or 3/4": $300 - Rental: $95
Please use this code to order: FRON-612K-AC04.

"Still burning . . . Confronting Ethnoviolence on Campus"
Marketing Coordinator
Instructional Technology
University of Maryland - Baltimore County
Baltimore, MD 21228-5398   Tel: 301/455-3686
Still burning is a two-part series examining issues of human relations and ethnoviolence (any incident of insensitivity or violence motivated by racial, religious or ethnic prejudice) from two points of view: Personal and institutional. The series focuses on the campus environment and offers preventive measures. The incidents depicted are based on actual occurrences on university campuses throught the country. This videotape is available in 1/2" VHS and 3/4" U-matic formats. Each part is 20 minutes in length.

"When Cultures Meet Face to Face: The Intercultural Experience"
Penfield Associates
P.O. Box 4493
Highland Park, NJ 08904   Tel: 201/932-8355
This 30-minute video, can be used as a crosscultural training tool for college and high school groups. International students are presented in four campus settings: (1) in the classroom, (2) making friends, (3) dealing with campus staff, and (4) on the job. Each of these four encounters between an international student and an American is presented twice. The second presentation of each encounter includes the projected "thoughts" of those engaged in the encounter. This segment can be used to encouraged participant involvement and discussion. The 1/2" VHS video costs $85.00, plus shipping. A training booklet with tips for novice trainers and activities is included with the video or may be purchased separately for $15.00 plus shipping.

CHAPTER 4

Introductory Activities

The activities included in this chapter can be used during your retreat. They include introductory, warm up, values, confrontation, Minority history and similar activities.

Introduce Your Partner

Have each participant pair up with another person, ideally someone he/she doesn't know at all. This process can be speeded up by asking them to count off one, two, one, two, ...(This can also be varied by sex or race by having women be all ones and men all twos and pairing off and having whites be all ones and minorities all twos and pairing off).

Give all persons a 5 by 8 inch card and have them interview each other for five minutes. This activity is normally done on the bus ride, but in case you used other means of transportation, this activity is a good one to start off with. Give them the following items to be included in the interview:

-name, and /or nickname, ethnic/racial background, job, school, travel, hobbies/interest

-experiences with different racial groups

-why they came

-what they hope to get out of this activity

-one thing (activity, food, leisure..) they like and one thing they dislike.

When the time is up have everyone form a circle. Give each person 2-3 minutes to introduce his or her partner to the total group. Members of the group can ask additional questions or clarify questions of the person being introduced. The facilitator should participate in this exercise as well to emphasize a community atmosphere.

Greet to the Beat

This is a fun way to loosen participants up and have them meet each other. Have the group form a Soul Train line (two lines facing each other). With medium to fast paced music playing in the background, have two people at a time walk or dance down the line introducing themselves. Both lines should sway to the music. When the two people reach the end of the line they reverse positions and go back up the opposite line and introduce themselves to people in that line. When the couple reaches the top of the line the entire group shouts welcome Tom & Mary (whatever their names may be and applauds). Then the next couple starts.

Introductory Activities

This process is repeated until everyone has had a chance to go down and up the Soul Train line. Encourage participants to be creative when they go up and down the line.

Mingle and Meet

Give each person in the group a 3" by 5" index card. Have them record the following information on the card: 1) their name, 2) their astrological sign and, 3) finish the sentence "I am here because . . ".

Have them tape or pin the card to their clothing in such a way that participants can read their cards. Tell participants they have two minutes to walk around the room, read as many cards as they can and introduce themselves. This exercise works well in getting people to talk about themselves. It helps put people at ease since everyone has to answer the same questions and talk about their astrological sign.

Misc. Introductory Activities

1. Have participants tell their names. Next have them pass an object such as a ball and have them say something using the word ball as they pass it around. Only the person with the ball can speak.

2. Have the participants repeat their names and use an adjective describing how they feel.

3. Have persons get together according to zodiac signs, home states, birth dates, etc. and introduce themselves to the group members.

4. Have participants pile name tags on the floor and have each person grab a name tag other than his/her own and find the owner introducing him/herself in the process.

5. Make up cards with numerous things for the participants to do, say, or pantomime and have each one select a card and do whatever the card says.

6. Have participants pile their left shoes in a pile and have each person grab a shoe that's not his/her own and put the shoe on the owner's foot and introduce themselves.

Warm Up Activities

Finger Match

Have participants form groups of three forming a small circle. When the facilitator says ready, set, go using one hand only, each group is to try to extend exactly ten fingers out (of course there can be no talking among group members). If one person extends say 5 fingers and someone else four and the third person

Warm Up Activities

two, obviously they have extended more than ten fingers. The facilitator repeats the instructions ready, set, go until one group has extended exactly ten fingers. This game usually generates enthusiasm and participants normally shout or applaud loudly when they've succeeded in getting ten fingers. This activity can be stopped after the first group extends ten fingers or groups can take their seats after they reach ten through a process of elimination. Either way this makes for a fun energizer that can help get the day off on a good foot.

Multicultural Groups

This activity should take place in a wide open space. All chairs, tables, etc. should be moved out of the way because participants will need to move around with their eyes closed in this exercise. Have participants form groups of four. (If there are an equal number of whites and minorities present each group should have two white and two minority members); otherwise base your mix on a percentage of the number in attendance.

Before participants form their groups inform them they are not to talk in the exercise, nor open their eyes. Their goal is to create a multi-cultural circle consisting of four people. Half of the group is to be white members and the other half, members of a racial minority group. As you might suspect, since participants can't talk or look in this activity, it gets very exciting. Expect a lot of touching and laughter. Allow participants about 5-10 minutes to form their groups.

After the time is up ask them how they were able to form a multi-cultural group. If they were unsuccessful ask them to explain why. This activity is a perfect lead in to a discussion about cultural differences, stereotypes, color blindness, etc. Spend some time discussing this activity.

Puzzle Game

Write fun messages or instructions on several sheets of paper (For example: Shake hands with everyone in your group, Feel the heads of all bald-headed persons, Hug all the males in your group, etc.). Cut the messages up so no more than two or three words appear on the paper. Mix all the parts of messages up and distribute randomly among the participants. Inform them that their words form a message when joined together with other words. They are to find the other words, complete the message and do whatever the message says. This activity can end when the first group completes its puzzle or continue until all groups have completed their puzzles.

Confrontation Exercises

Racial Fact Sheets

A. 1. Divide participants along racial lines.

2. Next have participants spend about 30 minutes compiling a one page fact sheet they would give an alien about Whites, Asians, Blacks, Indians and Hispanics. Emphasize the need for honesty as opposed to tact.

3. Also have each racial group create a fact sheet about themselves.

4. Have each group select a spokesperson.

5. Bring the groups back together and have the spokespersons read their fact sheets. Allow ample time for discussion, clarification and confrontation.

6. Conclude by having the group brainstorm what should be included on a fact sheet when describing a human being.

Controversial Statements

B. 1. Have participants discuss these statements:

a. All whites are racists!

b. Minorities should quit blaming whites for their problems and do something about it themselves!

c. I would not want to be an **Indian** (substitute any ethnic group) because...

d. I would not marry a **Asian** person (substitute any ethnic group) because...
    Encourage participants to be honest about their feelings.

Breaking In

C. 1. Have participants form a seven to nine person circle. Designate the circle as a white neighborhood.

2. Next designate someone as a black person to physically break into the circle.

3. Have the circle designated as a neighborhood lock arms and physically keep the black person out. (Since this exercise is a physical one and gets rough at times, remind the participants to show restraint).

4. After the black person has tried to break in, discuss this activity. Discuss what the white neighborhood must do to keep blacks out? How does it feel to have to force one's way into the neighborhood?

Confrontation Exercises

Cultural Exploration

Divide the participants along racial lines into groups of three. Tell the groups they are to spend about thirty minutes planning an activity they feel would interest someone of a different racial group. (Ideally this activity should be something that could actually be carried out). Tell them to write out (1-2 pages) why they selected this particular activity and why they feel someone who is racially different would enjoy it. After each group has finished writing their cross-cultural activity exchange papers and have the group the event was planned for evaluate the activity in terms of strengths/weaknesses, stereotypes and make suggestions as to how the affected group would have planned the activity differently.

Allow ample time for discussions. This exercise reveals a lot about participants values, sensitivities and perceptions of others. Another option is to allow the groups to actually conduct the activity during their free time and then discuss it afterwards.

This activity normally reveals the need to include impacted groups when planning cross cultural events. The various factors that must be considered usually surface during the discussion in a manner that illustrates the need for better communication and understanding. This is a good exercise to help participants reflect on their feelings about others who are culturally different.

Values Clarification Exercise

No Place to Study

Directions: Read the following to the participants. Have them discuss the values and assumptions that are implied in the story.

The setting is a college student union. Ralph, a black student, is concerned that no black studies courses are offered in his subject area. He goes through the regular procedures to obtain funds, approval, and a faculty member for a black studies course. Twenty black students sign up. Ralph goes to the student union director and asks if they can use the movie room on Thursday nights since that is the only time the professor is free. The movie room is also the only room in the union with audio-visual equipment. The student union director approves the request.

Thursday night arrives. The black students go to the movie room and find a group of white students watching Animal House. A heated discussion occurs. Charlie, a white student, yells out, "you damn niggers don't belong on this campus anyway."

Tom, a white student, believes that the black students should be allowed to use the movie room since it is the only place they have to meet. He does not say anything, however.

The black students leave. Ralph later goes to the student union director to explain what happened. The director replies, "I made a mistake. The movie room really serves a need for all students. Since there are only 20 students, find another place."

The next Thursday night the black students go to the movie room early and begin class. When white students arrive and demand to watch movies a fight breaks out, there are injuries and several hundred dollars worth of damage done to the movie room.

Discuss who is at fault? How should the situation have been handled? You can use the following values and assumptions to stimulate the discussion.

Values
* Black studies have a low priority-why do you think this is so ?
* Black studies mean violence
* White people can't be forced to integrate
* Black needs are unimportant
* It's a White problem

Assumptions
* Lack of understanding
* Denial of responsibility
* Minorities receiving special privileges
* Ignorance of legitimate minority demands

Values Clarification Exercise

What's Your Choice?

This exercise is designed to help participants clarify their values. Read the statements below and allow ample time for discussion. To be successful in your discussions help participants realize that to clarify their values they have to understand how they came to prize their beliefs and behaviors, how they selected their beliefs and behaviors and how to act on their beliefs.

1. If you had to be born over, which would you rather be?
An American Black, An African Black, or a European Black.

2. Which death is the greatest loss?
Martin Luther King Jr., Jesus Christ, John F. Kennedy, Malcolm X.

3. Which would you have the easiest time introducing to your parents?
A homosexual friend, an interracial date, or a Nazi member?

4. Which would you prefer as a neighbor if there was only one house available in your neighborhood?
A white couple, a minority couple, or a foreign couple?

5. If it was your decision to make, what funds would you cut first?
Welfare, defense, or funds for education?

6. Who should get the longest sentence?
A robber, a murderer, or a rapist?

7. If you had to legalize a drug which would you choose?
Marijuana, Cocaine, or heroin?

The Fatal Choice

After their ship sank in heavy seas, eight survivors found themselves on a rubber raft that was gradually sinking because it could support only six adults. The eight survivors included a 65 year old white man, a Jewish doctor, a 25 year old blond woman, a black baby boy and his mother, a white sailor, a young black minister, and a convicted Indian murderer who was prior to the shipwreck, being transported to jail to serve a life sentence.

They all knew the raft would sink within a half hour if their weight wasn't reduced. Because they had been blown out of the main shipping lanes, there was almost no chance of being rescued for two or three days. Two people would have to be removed from the raft. The survivors talked it over, but no one would volunteer to jump overboard. Who should be forcibly removed from the raft? Why?

Values Clarification Exercise

Stereotyping

This activity should start off with a definition of stereotyping. Next the facilitator explains to the participants that the activity they will be engaging in will help determine whether they have any stereotypes at work. The facilitator continues by saying: "I will read some paragraphs and you stop me as soon as you get a mental picture of the people you think I am describing. Tell me who you see." The facilitator may want to start with the descriptions below:

1. A group of people are gathered around a table. They are having a great time, drinking wine and laughing loudly. The music playing in the background sounds like an opera. The robust mother yells in an accented voice at her son for dropping spaghetti on the carpet. What ethnic group am I talking about?

2. Walking down the city street, I observed some people sitting in front of a housing project listening to loud music and doing fancy dance steps ever so often. A Cadillac pulls up, a good looking woman gets out and I hear someone say, "What's happening momma?" What ethnic group do you see?

3. I'm sitting in the living room of a family. The children are well behaved and polite. They bow when they greet the grandfather. The tell me they are having rice for dinner and ask whether I prefer chopsticks or a fork. What ethnic group do you see?

4. While stopping to fill my car with gas, a pick up truck stops near the tank across from mine. I can't help but notice the gun in the window and the confederate flag in full display. A thin hairy man with a tattoo on his arm and a "pot gut" gets out of the truck and says, "Hey boy fill'er up!" What do you see?

The participants will probably identify the examples mentioned as follows: Example #1 Italians, #2 Blacks, #3 Asians and #4 Red neck/poor white.

The facilitator should then lead the group into a discussion of stereotypes. The questions listed can be used to stimulate the discussion.

1. Could these examples apply to other groups than the ones you've identified?

2. What did you find out about your stereotypes?

3. Would your stereotype determine how you might treat people?

4. How do you think you acquired your stereotypes?

Stereotyping

5. What do you plan to do about your stereotypes?

As a follow up have the participants write a paragraph on a stereotype they may have. Have them read it out loud and discuss why it is a stereotype. Continue the discussion.

Sensitivity Exercises

The Blind Sensitivity Game

1. Have the group pair off in teams of two.
Have one member close his/her eyes while being led around the room by the partner. This exercise is to build up a certain level of trust, to talk about dependency and to experience blindness for a brief period.

2. Repeat the exercise having the pairs trot around the room. Discuss.

3. Have everyone close their eyes and walk to the other side of the room. Discuss.

Blind Communication

1. Have the participants form two circles.

2. Have each circle count off beginning with 1, 2, 3, etc.

3. Next have each circle mix the numbers up so they will be out of order.

4. Then have both circles close their eyes, not speak and pretend that they can't hear.

5. Finally, when you say go, have both circles try to get back in numerical order with out talking, speaking, or looking.

6. Have them clap their hands when they feel they are back in order.

7. Then announce the winner.

8. Discuss this activity. Ask them what they felt the purpose of this activity was (to stress memory or *communication*).

Sensitivity Exercises

Jokes as Put Downs

Specific Learning Objective:
For the participants to recognize racist, sexist, and ethnic jokes as hurtful put downs.

Procedure:

1. Begin activity by asking questions below. Discuss these orally:
a) What is a joke?
b) Should a joke put down individuals or groups of people?
c) In what ways might a joke put down individuals or groups of people? Give some examples.
d) Have you ever been the butt of a joke? How did you feel in that situation? (Good, bad, dumb, or indifferent)?

2. Give participants a handout of three to six jokes. (see jokes in this section).

3. Have participants answer the following questions about the jokes provided them on the handout.
a) Who are the characters or individuals who are represented?
b) What did the joke say negatively or positively about the individual or group?
c) What emotions might the individual/group that is the brunt of the joke feel? Try to put yourself into that individual/group person's shoes.

4. Have participants tell one ethnic joke that they've heard.

5. As a culminating activity offer the following suggestions about how to check out a joke: Whenever you are about to tell a joke instead of using Jews, Blacks, or Polish people, women, native people, etc., as the character(s) in your joke, substitute "I" and/or "we" or "My friends" and "I" and/or "my family" to see whether you like what you heard about yourself or those that you care about. Try to refrain from telling ethnic jokes.

"Jokes"

1. Q: Why are poor whites found by trash cans?
   A: Because that's where they go window shopping.

2. Q: Why was a black man the only male survivor of the Titanic?
   A: He was the only one that could use his lips as a raft.

3. Q: Do you know how Chinese select names for their kids?
   A: By dropping coins onto a metal floor and listening to the sounds! Ding Dang, Twang Twong ....

Sensititvity Exercises

"Jokes"

Are You Six Feet Tall?

4. Q: What does a tongueless female dog have in common with a Blond?
   A: They're both dumb bitches.

This activity will show how the groups to which you belong help define who you are.

Procedure:

1. Split participants up into two groups: those who are six feet tall, and those who are under six feet.

2. For the purpose of this activity, pretend that all short people have the following traits:
a) ignorant   c) boring
b) homely looking   d) clumsy

3. The two groups should meet separately for 10-15 minutes. The tall people must decide how to treat the others. The short people must decide how they expect to be treated by the people over six feet. They must also decide how they will respond to that treatment.

4. For about 30 minutes tall people must treat the short people in the way they decided. The short people must respond to that treatment in whatever way they feel is appropriate and realistic.

5. Talk about what happened and how you felt about it.
a) How did it feel to be a member of your group?
b) How realistic do you think your group experience was?
c) How do you think your group helped you to define who you are?

6. What are the advantages and disadvantages of the group you belong to in real life.

Exclusion and Discrimination

> **A. Objective:** To help participants understand the impact that exclusion has on individuals who are not allowed to participate.

Activity and Discussion

Tell the participants they are eligible to earn three privileges if they qualify for the rules you have established. The three privileges are:

1. They don't have to wash dishes during the retreat.

2. They can be the first in line to eat at the retreat.

3. They can can sleep later than others at the retreat.

The rules they must qualify for are:

1. Be taller than 5'5"

2. Possess a driver's license

3. Be a male

After the students learns what it takes to qualify for the privileges, you can expect a lot of dissension and charges of being unfair (i.e., discrimination). This should lead into a lively discussion of what it means to be left out for reasons people have little control over. This activity also allows for role playing having the students who qualify for the privileges defend their selection. The discussion can be enlarged to include other forms of discrimination.

> **B. Objective:** The students should be able to determine appropriate ways to handle discriminatory situations. Read the situations below and discuss.

Situations--

1. Tom Stanley has just been hired as a rental agent to rent apartments in a large apartment complex. On his desk he finds a policy manual that lists policy #1 as follows: DO NOT rent any apartments to "Hippies." What should he do?

2. Mary Tolen gets beaten up by a neighborhood gang for having a Black friend over to visit. What should she do?

Exclusion and Discrimination

3. Charlie Goldberg wants to join a fraternity but it discriminates against Jews. He's Jewish. What should he do?

4. Susan Harris wants to try out for the boys basketball team but her parents are opposed to this. The coach wants her to try out but the boys resent it. What should she do?

5. Harold Tyler is really attracted to Jan Lockman and wants very badly to take her out on a date. The problem is that he is Black and she is White and their parents don't approve. What should they do?

> **C. Objective:** The students should be able to think through the myriad of issues city planners and concerned citizens must address to resolve housing problems.

Break the class up into small groups of between 5-7 people. Give each group the following written assignment:

Your group has just been appointed by the mayor as an advisory council to the City Planning Department. The Mayor expects you to come up with several sites for the city to consider in building low income housing.

The city is divided into four areas. Area A is considered the poor section of the city. Mostly Blacks and Hispanics live there. Most people call it a ghetto. Area B is the working class neighborhood. Blue collar whites and a few Minorities live in this section. Area C is where the professional class lives and Area D is where the wealthy live. Area D is totally opposed to low income housing and will fight against any effort to locate sites in their area. Area C, although not opposed to low income housing, will support it only if it is located in areas A and B.

Area B residents feel their neighborhood is already deteriorating and they believe if additional low income units are built their property values will go down. They also feel these houses are being built at their expense so they are opposed to low income housing. Area A residents want low income housing units badly but want them built in another area because the ghetto is too crowded. They understand the opposition from other segments of the city but vow to do whatever is necessary to get out of the overcrowded conditions.

What will you recommend to the mayor and the City Planning Department? What issues must be considered before you make your recommendation? Allow the groups about forty-five

**Exclusion and
Discrimination**

minutes to discuss the issues. Have each group select a spokesperson to share with the entire class what site that group will recommend to the mayor.

After each group has reported, have a general discussion about the issues raised by the students.

Half of a person's free time had to be spent with someone of a different "race"

African American History Test

True or False

1.____ The Baptist Church was the first African American denominational church for Blacks.

2.____ The first black heavyweight champion of the world was Jack Jones when he defeated Tommy Burnes.

3.____ Alonzo Pietro, the navigator of the Nina, one of Columbus's ships, was a Black man.

4.____ Matthew Henson accompanied Admiral Robert E. Peary as the co-discoverer of the South pole.

5.____ The Freedmen's Bureau was created by congress in 1865 to establish schools and improve the living conditions of free slaves and impoverished whites.

6.____ The term "Jim Crow" is the name of an old Negro song.

7.____ Negro is a term invented by the English to describe black slaves.

8.____ "Lift Every Voice and Sing" written by James Weldon Johnson is considered to be the Black National Anthem.

9.____ The Niagara Movement, forerunner to the NAACP met in Canada in 1905 because hotels on the New York state side of the falls refused Blacks.

10.___ Martin Luther King Jr. was the first Black to win the Nobel Peace Prize.

Completion

1._____ won four gold medals in the 1936 Olympics and angered Adolph Hitler with his impressive victories.

2._____ helped write the plans in 1793 for what is now Washington D.C. He was also a Mathematician and noted astronomer.

3._____ created a national back-to-Africa movement called the Universal Negro Improvement Association.

4._____ was a scientist who discovered nearly three hundred products from the peanut.

5._____ was the first state to legally recognize slavery.

African American History Test

Matching

1.____Founder of the first African Methodist Episcopal Church in 1787.

2.____First African American to publish an Almanac in the U.S.

3.____First Black woman to be named an ambassador in the U.S. She was appointed by former President Lyndon B. Johnson to Luxembourg in 1965.

4.____First person to die in the Boston Massacre on March 5, 1770.

5.____Founded a permanent settlement in Chicago in 1779.

6.____Ashnum Institute, founded by the Presbyterians in 1854 as a College for Blacks in Pennsylvania is now called_____.

7.____Fraternity founded at Cornell University in 1906.

8.____Organized anti-lynching societies throughout the U.S. and wrote a study of lynching, entitled-*The Red Record*.

9.____Introduced blood plasma on the battlefield and established the American Red Cross blood bank. Later he bled to death because white southern hospitals refused to admit him.

10.___Known as the "Messenger of Allah", he founded the Black Muslims.

A. Omega Psi Phi Fraternity
B. Dr. W.E.B. DuBois
C. Duke Ellington
D. Malcolm X
E. Elijah Muhammad
F. Charles Drew
G. Ida Bell Wells
H. Alpha Phi Alpha Fraternity

I. Barbara Jordan
J. James Weldon Johnson
K. Lincoln University
L. Jackson State University
M. Jean Baptiste Point duSable
N. Crispus Attucks
O. Patricia Roberts Harris
P. Benjamin Banneker
Q. Richard Allen

African American History Test

Answers

1. True
2. False (Jack Johnson)
3. True
4. False (north pole)
5. True
6. True, According to the book *Famous First Facts about Negroes*, the song dates back to 1838. It wasn't until later that it came to denote discrimination practices.
7. False, It is derived from the Spanish word and Portuguese word meaning black, although later adopted by the English.
8. True
9. True
10. False, Ralph J. Bunche was the first for negotiating an armistice between Israel and its Arab neighbors.

1. Jesse Owens
2. Benjamin Banneker
3. Marcus Garvey
4. Dr. George Washington Carver
5. Massachusetts

1. Q Richard Allen
2. P Benjamin Banneker
3. O Patricia Roberts Harris
4. N Cripus Attucks
5. M Jean Baptiste Point duSable
6. K Lincoln University
7. H Alpha Phi Alpha Fraternity
8. G Ida Bell Wells
9. F Dr. Charles Drew
10. E Elijah Muhammad

Asian American History Test

True/False

___ 1. The internment of Japanese Americans during World War II was supported by president Franklin D. Roosevelt.

___ 2. Chinese Americans make up the largest Asian American group in the U.S..

___ 3. There was a Japanese settlement in California as early as 1869.

___ 4. The first Chinese immigrants who came to the U.S. did not work on the railroads.

___ 5. To the Chinese, New Year represents everyone's birthday.

___ 6. The Chinese New Year usually begins anytime between March 20th and April 15th.

___ 7. Feng-shui is the belief in giving a packet of good luck money wrapped in red paper.

___ 8. Most Christian religions are not found in Asian cultures.

___ 9. The traditional Chinese Temple is found in almost every Chinese settlement.

___ 10. Buddhism is not a formal religion with priests, prayer, images and a vast array of gods.

___ 11. Chinese were reported in the U.S. as early as 1820.

___ 12. The Chinese almost single-handedly built the Pacific portion of the transcontinental railroad.

___ 13. In the 1974 Supreme Court Decision, Lau vs Nichols, the Chinese opposed bilingual education.

___ 14. When congress passed the Chinese Exclusion Act in 1882 it was the first time the U.S. denied entry based on national origin.

___ 15. Asian Culture did not stress secret societies and self reliance.

___ 16. The Nisei are known as the last generation of Americans of Japanese ancestry.

___ 17. Asian Americans are often referred to as "Model" minorities.

___ 18. Sukiyaki is a Japanese word meaning, how are you?

**Asian American
History Test**

True/False

Multiple Choice

___ 19. Most Japanese Americans who are Buddhist belong to the Jodo Shinshu Sect.

___ 20. Hanamatsuri is the day on which Buddhists celebrate the birth of Buddha.

1. Buddha-Dharma is ___
   (a) the teachings of Judo
   (b) the practice of oriental cooking
   (c) the teaching of the Buddha
   (d) the wife of the Buddha

2. The art of bonsai refers to ___
   (a) Japanese silk screening
   (b) Chinese wrestling
   (c) the growing of trees to exact replicas of large trees which grow in the forest
   (d) none of the above

3. The Koto is ___
   (a) a Korean word for house
   (b) a 13 string instrument used in Japan for many years
   (c) the newest Oriental dance to hit the west coast
   (d) the Vietnamese national anthem

4. This word sometimes means a japanese ghetto ___
   (a) Nihon machi
   (b) Sakana
   (c) Kanji
   (d) ghettuloheli

5. Third generation Japanese are called ___
   (a) Issei
   (b) Nisei
   (c) Yonsei
   (d) Sansei

**Asian American
History Test**

Answers

1. True	11. True
2. True	12. True
3. True	13. False
4. True	14. True
5. True	15. False
6. False	16. False
7. False	17. True
8. False	18. False
9. True	19. True
10. False	20. True

1. c
2. c
3. b
4. a
5. d

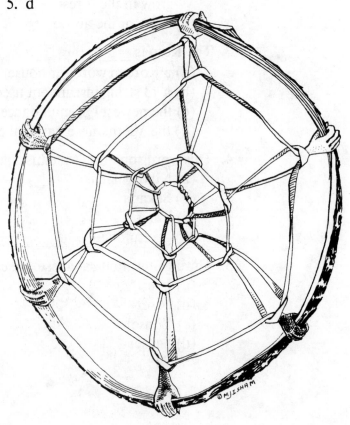

Chicano History Test

Taking this test should give you some idea of how much or how little you know about Chicano Culture and History. (Circle your answers)

1. The term "Chicano" refers to:
    a. "Militant" Mexican Americans
    b. Latinos who reject their culture
    c. Mexican Americans who desire the benefit of two cultures

2. The treaty of Guadalupe Hildago ceded to the United States what is now known as:
    a. the state of Texas
    b. the state of New Mexico
    c. the state of California
    d. the southwestern United States

3. Cinco de Mayo is a Mexican holiday which commemorates:
    a. Mexico's independence from France
    b. the battle of Puebla
    c. the death of the Frito Bandito
    d. the decline of the Diaz regime

4. Mexican culture has been influenced by which of the following cultures?
    a. Aztec
    b. Spanish
    c. Inca
    d. Indian
    e. all of the above

5. The first "wetbacks" crossed into America:
    a. at Ciudad Juarez in 1846
    b. at Tiajuana in 1922
    c. at Plymouth Rock in 1620
    d. at Nuevo Laredo in 1882

6. The Chicano equivalent of a "ghetto" is:
    a. el gato
    b. el barrio
    c. el rancho grande
    d. la tierra

Chicano History Test

7. A frajo is a:
   a. short handled hoe
   b. car
   c. cigarette
   d. pachuco

8. Chicanos in the United States average_____years of education.
   a. 9.3
   b. 5.0
   c. 12.2

9. Mysticism is used in Chicano culture to control behavior of children:
   a. hardly at all
   b. to a large degree
   c. never

10. A curandera is a:
    a. healer
    b. witch
    c. curious person

11. La Llorona and El Coco are recognized by almost all Chicano children to be
    a. benevolent persons
    b. animals
    c. bad persons

12. The 12th of December is:
    a. Cesar Chavez's Birthday
    b. The day of the Virgin of Guadalupe
    c. The anniversary of "pachuco" riots

13. La jura refers to:
    a. an Anglo jury
    b. a judge
    c. the cops
    d. a lawyer

14. To Chicanos their term Carnal means:
    a. brother
    b. butcher
    c. sports car
    d. enemy

Chicano History Test

15. Macho refers to:
    a. being chauvinistic
    b. being manly and honorable
    c. being a disloyal person
    d. being courteous

16. A tio taco is a:
    a. Mexican dish
    b. individual who rejects his culture
    c. Cuban
    d. an uncle from Spain

17. The most valued institution in Chicano Culture is:
    a. the educational institution
    b. the religious institution
    c. the political institution
    d. the family

18. The Chicano family is usually comprised of:
    a. parents and children
    b. parents, children, and relatives
    c. parents, children, and grandparents
    d. parents, children, relatives, and friends

19. Many Chicano parents feel their children will be severely handicapped by:
    a. erratic school attendance
    b. knowing and speaking spanish
    c. influences of Chicano culture
    d. learning both English and Spanish

20. Some teachers view the major handicap to be overcome by Chicano students as:
    a. culture conflicts
    b. lack of English-speaking ability
    c. short attention spans
    d. innate stupidity

Chicano History Test

Answers

1. c The term Chicano is a concept which many Mexican Americans identify with because it gives them a feeling of pride. It identifies them as being proud of their cultural heritage.

2. d The treaty of Guadalupe Hildago was signed by the United States and Mexico in 1848. With this treaty, Mexico accepted the RIO Grande as the Texas border and ceded the Southwest (which incorporates the present day states of Arizona, California, New Mexico, Utah, Nevada, and parts of Colorado) to the U.S. in return for $15 million.

3. b This celebration is in reference to a battle in which a small Mexican Army defeated a French Army Battalion. Cinco de Mayo celebrations are still commemorated in Mexico and all over the United States where there are a significant number of Chicanos.

4. e The Mexican heritage is one that is often referred to as Mestizo or "mixed". A number of different people have influenced what is known as "Mexican Culture" today.

5. c The term "wetback" is often used to refer to illegal Mexican aliens entering the United States. However,from the Chicano's point of view, the first "wetbacks" to enter this country were the pilgrims who crossed over on the May Flower.

6. b To Chicanos their neighborhood is known as el barrio.

7. c The term frajo is a slang word for cigarette which is commonly used in the barrio.

8. a This is a fluctuating figure that rises and falls from year to year. However,it should be stressed that Chicanos have the highest drop-out rate and the lowest educational level achievement of all groups of people in the United States.

9. b Traditionally, Chicano culture is very superstitious and parents utilize this belief to control their children.

10. a The curandera is a person who is able to relieve people of their physical sickness. Many elderly Chicano people do not believe in the "doctor" as they are known in this country. They prefer to be attended by the curandera or healer.

11. c La Llorona and El Coco are a couple of the superstitious characters utilized by parents to control the behavior of their children.

Chicano History Test

Answers

12. b Chicanos are a very religious people. The 12th of December is the day of the most patron saint of the Chicano people -The day of the virgin of Guadalupe.

13. c La jura is a slang term for "the cop" which every Chicano who resides in el barrio is well aware.

14. a Carnal simply means brother. It is usually used as a greeting between males.

15. b In Mexican culture to be Macho is to be manly and honorable. It incorporates a quite different meaning than is associated with the term here in the U.S.

16. b Many individuals reject their culture due to the educational system in this country. Chicanos have been taught that their culture is inferior and that the Anglo American culture is superior. Therefore, many Mexican Americans (especially second and third generations) cannot identify with their cultural heritage and the term Chicano.

17. d Chicano families are traditionally very, very close. The total Chicano existence revolves around the family.

18. d The Chicano family encompasses the extended type of family lifestyle which incorporates close friends. These close friends are usually referred to as "compadres" and "comadres".

19. b Many Chicano parents believe that their children will be handicapped if they are allowed to learn and speak spanish. Many Chicano parents want their children to succeed in school and they believe that knowing and speaking spanish will hinder rather than enhance their children's education.

20. b Many teachers are not aware of the cultural conflicts that Chicano children are confronted with when they first enter the educational system in this country. The children are accustomed to a particular lifestyle and when exposed to the "white middle class" surroundings they become disorganized and must try and adjust to their new environment. Teachers must become aware that it is more than just language conflicts that hinder Chicano children from learning -- it is the entire cultural diffierences.

Chicano History Test

Answers

How did you score?
For each correct answer give yourself 5 points.

90-100   Your are probably a Chicano.

80-89   Your are very aware of Chicano culture.

70-79   Contact your nearest Multicultural Education Center.

0-69   Your are culturally deprived.

© 1979 Henry Villareal

Native American History Test

True/False

	T	F	
1)	__	__	Scalping was a common Indian practice.
2)	__	__	The Political leaders of Indian Nations were known to their people as "Chief".
3)	__	__	The BIA was once a branch of the War Department.
4)	__	__	Indians were primarily nomadic people.
5)	__	__	Prior to the European invasion, cancer, syphilis, and tooth decay were virtually unknown on the North American continent.
6)	__	__	IHS stands for the Indian Health Service.
7)	__	__	Individual States are authorized to enter into treaties with Indian Nations by a special constitutional amendment.
8)	__	__	The Native American Church worships mescalito, the spirit god of peyote.
9)	__	__	A "snowsnake" is a reptile indigenous to cold climates.
10)	__	__	Gambling was first introduced to Indians in 1803 near Las Vegas, Nevada.
11)	__	__	AIM refers to "Allied Indian Manufacturers".
12)	__	__	Tuberculosis is virtually unknown in the U.S. today.
13)	__	__	Chicle, the chewy ingredient in bubble gum, was first introduced by Indians.
14)	__	__	"Manifest Destiny" is the belief that white men are ordained by god to own and control the North American Continent.
15)	__	__	Of the 371 major treaties signed by the U.S. and Indian Nations, 371 have been broken.

Multiple Choice

1) Which of the following is not an Indian invention?
   ___ Canoe
   ___ Kayak
   ___ Parka
   ___ Tomahawk

**Native American
History Test**

Multiple Choice

2) Of the four main staples in world food, which of the following two were first domesticated by Indians?

___ Rice

___ Corn

___ Wheat

___ Potatoes

3) The Words "Kemo Sabe", popularized by the Lone Ranger's sidekick Tonto, means:

___ White Friend

___ Blue Eyes

___ Honky

___ Nothing at all

4) The phrase "The only good Indian is a dead Indian" is attributed to:

___ Gen. Philip Sheridan

___ Gen. Wm. T. Sherman

___ Col. Henry B. Carrington

___ Lt. Col. Geo. A. Custer

5) Which of the following was not a member of the League of Six Nations (Iroquois Confederacy)?

___ Oneida

___ Seneca

___ Kiowa

___ Onondaga

6) Which of the Following major colleges was first instituted primarily to educate Indians?

___ Yale

___ Harvard

___ Dartmouth

___ Princeton

Native American History Test

Matching

1. ___ Geronimo		A	Iroquois prophet
2. ___ Wovoka		B	Hunkpapa Sioux Medicine Man
3. ___ Clarence Tinker		C	Osage: General, U.S. Air Force
4. ___ Oshkosh		D	Sac & Fox: 1912 Olympic
5. ___ Dekanawida			Decathlon Champ
6. ___ Jim Thorpe		E	Kaw-Osage: Vice-President,
7. ___ Eli S. Parker			1928-33
8. ___ Charles Curtis		F	Chiricahua Apache Medicine Man
9. ___ Sitting Bull		G	Menominee Chief
		H	Seneca: 1st Indian BIA
			Commissioner 1869-71
		I	Paiut Medicine Man

Matching

Tribe		Region	
1. ___ Seminole		A	Eastern Woodlands
2. ___ Miami		B	Southeast
3. ___ Yakima		C	Great Plains
4. ___ Pawnee		D	Northwest
5. ___ Arapaho		E	Southwest
6. ___ Apache			
7. ___ Potawatomi			
8. ___ Creek			
9. ___ Hopi			
10. ___ Salish			

Matching

Date		Event	
1. ___ 1492		A	Discovery of Columbus in Caribbean
2. ___ 1754		B	Dawes General Allotment Act
3. ___ 1838		C	Wounded Knee I
4. ___ 1864		D	Indian Reorganization Act
5. ___ 1870		E	Sand Creek Massacre
6. ___ 1887		F	Little Big Horn Victory
7. ___ 1890		G	Termination Act
8. ___ 1934		H	French & Indian Wars
9. ___ 1953		I	Trail of Tears
10. ___ 1972		J	Self-Determination Act

Native American History Test

Answers

True/False

1) False

Scalping was instituted by the Dutch in the 17th century. Settlers were paid a bounty on all scalps brought in; male scalps generally were paid more than female or children's scalps.

2) False

"Chief" is an Anglo-European Term. Many Indian Tribes have accommodated this word.

3) True

The BIA was transferred from the War Dept. to the Dept. of Interior in 1849.

4) False

Many Plains Indians followed the migrating aminals upon which they depended, but all Tribes have clearly defined territories, and most were permanently settled in towns and villages.

5) True

Pre-15th century North America was relatively free of these serious diseases.

6) True

The BIA controlled health services until 1955, when IHS was transferred to the Public Health Service under DHEW. No substantial changes were made, unfortunately.

7) False

The U.S. Government reserves sole right to enter into treaties; any State-Indian Tribe treaties are supposedly invalid. (1790 Non-Intercourse Act).

8) False

The Native American Church uses peyote as an aid to inducing visions, from where its individual members then derive names and direction.

9) False

A snowsnake is a game played by the Iroquois. The snowsnake itself is a long, narrow piece of wood, rounded at the front and tapering toward the rear.

10) False

Many Indian Tribes had a highly developed system of gambling.

11) False

AIM is the American Indian Movement, a political pressure group of militant young warriors.

12) False

Tuberculosis is the second major killer of Indians living on reservations, according to IHS statistics.

Native American History Test

Answers

True/False

13) True
Chicle was used by South American Indians many centuries before Wrigley patented it.

14) True
Manifest Destiny was the handiest justification for land acquisition and westward expansion.

15) True
Not one single documented treaty between the U.S. and Indians has ever been fully honored. "They made us many promises, more than I can remember, but they never kept but one; they promised to take our land, and they took it"
  -anonymous Indian.

Multiple Choice

1) The tomahawk was a french invention later copied and used extensively by Indians.

2) Corn and Potatoes

3) No one knows where this phrase comes from; there are no known languages that this can be traced to-another Hollywood gimmick.

4) Gen. Sheridan's direct quote: "The only good Indians I ever saw were dead." The phrase was later simplified for layman's use.

5) The Six Nations were composed of: Oneida, Seneca, Tuscorora, Ononodaga, Cayuga, and Mohawk.

6) Dartmouth

Native American History Test

Answers

Matching

Name	Tribe - Region	Date - Event
1 - F	1 - B	1 - A
2 - I	2 - A	2 - H
3 - C	3 - D	3 - I
4 - G	4 - C	4 - E
5 - A	5 - C	5 - F
6 - D	6 - E	6 - B
7 - H	7 - A	7 - C
8 - E	8 - B	8 - D
9 - B	9 - E	9 - G
	10 - D	10 - J

© 1979 Chris Johns

American Indians shared aspects of their culture

**Puerto Rican
History Test**

1. Puerto Rico before the Spanish conquest was called
   a) Boriquen
   b) Caparra
   c) San Juan Bautista

2. The most important Puertorican painter of the eighteenth century
   was
   a) Jose Campeche
   b) Francisco Oller
   c) Lorenzo Homar

3. Eugenio Maria de Hostos was
   a) a doctor
   b) an engineer
   c) writer and philosopher

4. In what year was the Estado Libre Asociado of Puerto Rico
   (Commonwealth) established?
   a) 1898
   b) 1917
   c) 1952

5. During the Spanish conquest the first Puertorican settlement was
   called
   a) Caparra
   b) San German
   c) Viejo San Juan

6. The "cemi" is a
   a) kind of food
   b) a religious idol
   c) the skirt used by taino women.

7. The first Puertorican governor was
   a) Luis Munoz Marin
   b) Jesus T. Pinero
   c) Luis A. Ferre

8. The first elected Puertorican governor was
   a) Luis Munoz
   b) Jesus T. Pinero
   c) Antonio R. Barcelo

**Puerto Rican
History Test**

9. The "Grito de Lares" was held to
   a) protest against slavery
   b) protest against the United States invasion of the island
   c) gain independence form Spain

10. In what year was slavery abolished in Puerto Rico.
    a) 1872
    b) 1868
    c) 1821

11. The Puertorican national anthem is
    a) La Borinquena
    b) En mi Viejo San Juan
    c) El Jibarito

12. Rafael Hernandez was a
    a) governor
    b) singer
    c) musician

13. The first Puertorican elected to the congress of the United States
    was
    a) Mauricio Ferre
    b) Hernan Badillo
    c) Jamie Benitez

14. A great baseball player for Puerto Rico was
    a) Piculin
    b) Roberto Clemente
    c) Jose L. (Chegui) Torres

15. The author of "La Carreta" was
    a) Hector Campos Parsi
    b) Rafael Hernandez
    c) Rene Marquez

16. The best known composer of Puertorican "danzas" was
    a) Pablo Casals
    b) Sylvia Rexach
    c) Juan Morel Campos

17. Pedro Albizu Campos was a political leader in favor of
    a) independance for Puerto Rico
    b) anexation for Puerto Rico
    c) the Commonwealth of Puerto Rico

**Puerto Rican
History Test**

18. The slogan of the Popular Democratic Party has been since its beginnings
    a) "Que el pueblo decida"
    b) "El que a la palma se arrima buena sombra lo cobija"
    c) "Pan, tierra y libertad"

19. In Puerto Rico an annual festival of flowers is held in the town of
    a) Mayaguez
    b) Utuado
    c) Aibonito

20. Citizenship was extended to all Puertoricans by the Congress of the United States in the year of
    a) 1952
    b) 1917
    c) 1898

Puerto Rican History Test

Answers

1 - a
2 - a
3 - c
4 - c
5 - a
6 - b
7 - b
8 - a
9 - c
10 - a
11 - a
12 - c
13 - b
14 - b
15 - c
16 - c
17 - a
18 - c
19 - c
20 - b

Example of "table-tent" Invitation Sent to Student Leaders

Overview of the Retreat

Purpose

The purpose of a cultural retreat is to allow white and minority students an opportunity to explore racial/cultural issues in an isolated setting that is free of major distractions. Through a structured approach students are able to discuss, debate and contribute in ways that may help them discover, share and broaden their awareness of themselves in relationship to the multicultural world at large.

Program

Besides ethnic food, fun activities and the great outdoors, dynamic speakers have been asked to share the Black, Hispanic and Native American experience with students. Students will be able to engage these speakers and hear new ways to address old problems. In addition student lead committees will be asked to identify problems they feel the administration should concentrate on and share these concerns with the campus administration. Finally participants will be expected to answer the question, "Where do we go from here?"

— — — — — — — — — — — *Fold here* — — — — — — — — — —

Name of your campus

Date: October 14 - 16
Place: Lutherdale Bible Camp and Conference Center
Departure Time and Place: Friday, October 14 - 2:30 p.m.
in front of the campus bookstore. Please arrive a few minutes early.
Return Time and Date: Sunday, October 16 at 3 p.m.

Special Guests on Saturday:
Representatives from the campus administration

RSVP by October 1st

A fun and educational activity to help individuals appreciate diversity and experience cultural pluralism.

Addendum

Sample letter inviting student leaders to attend the retreat.

September 15, 1989

President
Student Organization
Your Campus

Dear:

During the weekend of October 14 - 16, forty student leaders from (your campus) will be participating in (your campus's) first cultural retreat. The retreat will be held at (your desired location).

At this retreat Asian, Black, Chicano, Indian and White students will have the opportunity to participate in workshops, group activities, games and entertainment provided by Black, Hispanic and Native American speakers. This event will allow students to not only explore cultural differences but also to discuss important issues that tend to block better race relations on campus. Please make sure your organization is represented at this event. I would like to be put on the agenda of your next meeting and answer any questions your organization might have. I will call you later this week. Although there may be another retreat offered in the spring (that will be open to other students), this first retreat is primarily for student leaders.

On behalf of the cultural retreat planning committe, we are asking the President and two other officers from your organization to attend this unique cultural experience. Please submit three names from your organization to me by September 27th. An official invitation will be sent to them along with complete information about the retreat.

With best regards,

(Your name), Chair
Cultural Retreat Planning Committee

Examples of Information Gathered from Group Sessions

Below are examples of pledges students made individually and in groups describing what they would do once they returned to campus.

Individual pledges

1. Communicate more often - verbally, smile, handshake, etc.

2. Continue Retreats - send out letters talking about previous retreats.

3. Judge a person for who they are, not for the color of their skin.

4. Learn and retain the names of speakers I have heard.

5. Have a T-shirt day where everyone who attended the retreat wears their T-shirt.

6. Promote involvement with student government and in the residence halls.

7. Attend more cultural workshops.

8. Suggest Residence Hall programming (educational and social).

Group pledges

1. Sponsor an all day Cultural Affairs Day with nationally known speakers.

2. Establish student mentors to help students adjust to campus life.

3. Work to make our campus's orientation multicultural.

4. Help to establish a Multicultural Center on campus.

5. Work to improve town-gown relations.

6. Meet with the curriculum committee and work with chancellor to mandate ethnic studies.

7. Stay on top of the Affirmative Action Committee and monitor its racial harassment policies. Request a specific deadline for completion of the policies.

8. Sponsor cultural food fest and other events.

9. Create a multicultural brochure to promote diversity.

Addendum

Examples of Information Gathered from Group Sessions

> Listed below are some examples of problems identified that Minorities face on predominantly white campuses.

Problems:

1. Communication
2. Stereotypes / Labeling - Eliminate term "minority"
3. Lack of cultural studies and opportunities.
4. Being singled out.
5. Police harassment
6. Lack of staff from different ethnic groups.
7. Racism - Faculty has lower expectations.
8. Together in class/divided once out.
9. Lack of interaction between majority and non-majority students socially.
10. No preparation for leadership.
11. Feel inhibited.
12. Adjustment
13. Fear of differences.

Solutions:

1. Have a cultural retreat during orientation.
2. Bring national minority speakers to campus.
3. Make ethnic studies mandatory.
4. Read books by non-majority authors.
5. Sponsor a retreat for all faculty.
6. Work to overcome cultural ignorance.
7. Change curriculum for undergraduate students.
8. Have the university sponsor cultural awareness training.
9. Town-gown committee, when can/will it be created.
10. Teach people to be assertive and express how they feel.
11. Approve a racial harassment policy.

Questions on racism that can be used after showing the video Racism 101

1. Is Affirmative Action responsible for the presence of minorities on campuses across the country?

2. What kinds of racial conflicts have occurred on our campus? Were they handled properly?

3. How does racial conflict build? What are its salient characteristics? How does it manifest itself?

4. Name names. List all the racist tags you have heard used on our campus. Describe the context in which they were used.

5. Do you feel racism is a serious problem on our campus?

6. What is your immediate response when you hear someone use racial slurs and/or when they are aimed at you? What is the response you would like to make?

7. A student in the film, Racism 101 states "Everyone has something to gain" in fighting racism. Is this true? What do you have to gain?

8. In your opinion what is needed, required to make a commitment to fight racism?

9. Is racial harmony really only a pipedream?

10. Can our university create racial harmony? What is the price you are willing to pay?

11. To effect change, do we need to confront? Do we need to be combative? What are the alternatives?

12. How do we share power?

13. Has racism been dealt with at our campus? Have you heard about the racial climate on our campus during the 60's, 70's? How would you characterize racial conditions at your campus in the 90's? Are things better, worse?

14. Who are your heroes? What are their stances on the racial question?

15. Should admission to a university be based on academic excellence or other factors such as talent in art, music, athletics?

Questions on Racism that can be used after video Racism 101

16. What do you think Martin Luther King, Jr. really wanted in his struggle for civil rights? What do minorities want?

17. Do minorities on our campus keep themselves separate, distinct? Do they tend to "weed" themselves out?

18. Where does resistance to assimilate, into the mainstream come from?

19. Do minorities exclude whites on our campus and vice versa? Why?

20. Can people change? Can institutions change? Why? Why not?

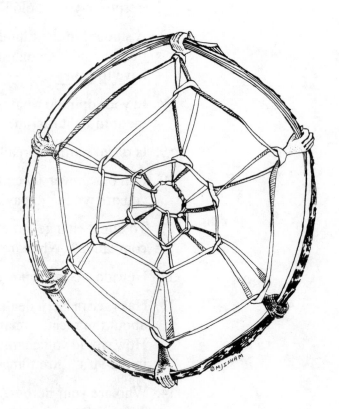

**Student Group
Guidelines**

> Here are some instructions for the student group brainstorming and feedback process that we will use during our Retreat. The first group will focus on the question "What problems do minority students face on our predominantly White campus?"

**Problems Minority
students face**

1. Have a member of the group record the brainstormed ideas of the group on the pieces of "banner paper" that will be provided.

2. Discuss the list you have brainstormed, and then select the top three problems.

3. Discuss how these problems and concerns may be addressed.

4. Select a member from your group who will serve as a spokesperson to present your suggestions to representatives of the campus administration.

5. Please keep the banner paper and the ideas that you have brainstormed. We would like to collect them, collate the information, and provide a complete listing to you at a later date.

**Where do we go from
here?**

> The second group will focus on "Where do we go from here?" The goal of this group is to suggest ways that we as individuals, and members of the organizations that we represent, can continue to promote the unity and the celebration of diversity that we have addressed at this retreat.

1. Select a member of the group to record comments that are to be brainstormed by the group.

2. Topics should be brainstormed in two areas:
   A. What can I as an individual do to promote unity and diversity among different cultural groups on campus?
   B. What can student organizations on campus do to promote unity and diversity among the different cultural groups on campus?

3. Select a spokesperson who will present your ideas in each area to retreat participants tomorrow.

4. Please feel comfortable in sharing all of your ideas with us so that we may collate information and compile a list of possible plans. We will share this information with all members of the retreat in the near future.

Addendum

Recipes

These recipes are examples of dishes we've served. Feel free to use them. We also recommend that you ask your attendees for suggestions of dishes as well. You may want to subsitute some of the dishes for more nutritional ones. Eat well!

Sample Cultural Retreat Menu

Native American Dinner
Corn Soup
Fry Bread
Acorn Squash
Berries
Beverage

Asian Dinner
Fried Rice
Soup
Vegetables
Fortune Cookies
Tea

Soul Food Dinner
Fried Chicken
Sweet Corn
Corn Bread
Greens
Sweet Potato Pie
Beverage

Mexican (Chicano) Dinner
Barbacoa
Frijoles
Arroz
Tortillas
Beverage

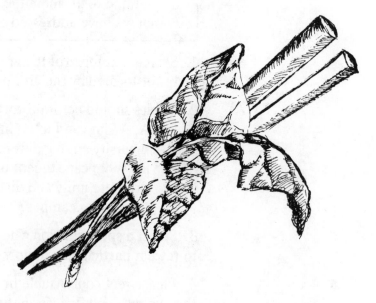

Native American Recipes

Venison Corn Soup

Place odd pieces of venison (rib, shoulder, neck) in a large kettle with three to four cups of dried corn and enough water to cover the ingredients. Season as desired. Simmer until tender.

Dandelion Greens

Gather greens before blooming. Wash them well. Add a small amount of water and simmer. Add seasonings (salt, butter, oil, and/or vinegar). Serve hot.

AH-GEE-DAH-MO (Squirrel Soup)

Cut up three to four squirrels. Cover with water and add 1 tablespoon of salt and onions if desired. Simmer until meat falls off bones. Remove and add any vegetables on hand (dried corn, carrots, potatoes), and seasonings. Thicken with flour. Cook until tender.

Squaw Bread

1 pint of sweet milk or cream

2 tbsp. of baking powder

1 tsp. of salt

1 tbsp. of shortening

Enough flour to make dough

Mix, knead and roll out to any thickness desired. Cut in pieces and fry in deep fat.

Milk weed

2 - 3 pounds of milk weed

1/2 pound of salt pork

Wash the milk weed and cut up quite fine along with the meat. Add seasonings. Simmer for about 2 1/2 to 3 hours until tender.

Addendum

**Native American
Recipes**

Wecemize Wesne

4 cups of parched corn, ground quite fine

1 cup of suet

2 cups of dried wild choke cherries

Mix together, let stand until it is firm, slice for dessert.

Corn Soup

white corn

lima or pinto beans

salt pork or pork hocks

beef (optional)

Wash corn (soak overnight and rinse several times). Cube meat. Boil meat, add corn and beans and boil for about one hour.

Fry Bread

4 cups of flour

2 cups of water

3 tbsp. of baking soda

2 tbsp. of dry milk

1 tbsp. of shortening

2 tsp. of salt

Sift all dry ingredients. Mix shortening. Add water slowly. Knead until soft. Mold, deep fry, drain and serve. Makes enough for six or seven people. Both corn soup and fry bread can be made in several different ways. The two recipes have been used in preparing the retreat's Native American food dinner. To complete the meal, wild rice (when available) and berries can be served along with any wild meat (venison, rabbit, squirrel, etc.). Herb tea or water will complement the meal.

Mexican Recipes

Barbacoa

2 lbs. boneless chuck roast

salt and pepper to taste

1 cup water

Place roast in slow cooker with water. Sprinkle salt and pepper over roast. Set slow cooker at low temperature. For very tender juicy meat, cook for at least 6 - 10 hours. Makes about 3 to 4 servings.

Arroz (rice)

1 cup rice

2 tbsp. cooking oil

1/2 cup chopped onion

1/4 cup chopped green pepper

1/2 cup cut tomatoes (fresh or canned)

1 tbsp. cumin

1 small can tomato sauce

1 cup water

salt and pepper to taste

In a frying pan at low heat, place cooking oil and rice stirring slowly until rice turns golden brown. Add onions, tomatoes, green pepper and garlic. Stir. Add seasonings (salt, pepper, cumin). Saute about one minute, add tomato sauce and water. Bring to a boil then simmer for about 20 to 25 minutes or until water evaporates. (An additional 1/2 cup of water may be needed). Check occasionally but do not stir. Makes 4 to 6 servings.

Frijoles (beans)

1 lb. pinto beans

1/2 cup chopped onion

1/4 lb. salt pork or bacon

1/2 cup chopped tomato

2 sprigs cilantro

Addendum

Mexican Recipes

1 clove garlic

chopped jalepeno (optional)

salt and pepper to taste

2 qts. water

Soak pinto beans in cold water overnight. Rinse pinto beans and set to boil at medium flame in two quarts of water. After boiling for about 15 - 20 minutes, reduce heat. Add remaining ingredients. Cook for 1 hr to 1 1/2 hr, until beans are tender.

Caldo de Res (Beef Soup)

4-5 lbs. of soup bones

2-3 potatoes cubed

1/2 head of cabbage

1/2 large onion, chopped

2 fresh (or one can) tomatoes, chopped

1/2 cup of rice (salt and pepper to taste)

Put soup bones, cabbage, onion, and tomato in about three quarts of water to cook over low heat. Let simmer for about one hour. Then add rice and potatoes and cook for an additional 15 to 20 minutes. Make sure meat is tender; if not cook slowly without stirring, for an additional 10 - 20 minutes.

Taquitos de Carnitas

1 doz. corn tortillas

2-3 lbs. of desired meat, cubed

Slowly, using low heat, brown flour coated meat. Add salt and pepper and if desired, onions. Steam heat corn tortillas until soft, roll meat into tortilla and hold in place with took pick.

Mexican Recipes

Guacamole

Peel and mash avocadoes in small bowl. Add chopped onions and tomatoes, salt and pepper to taste. If desired mild chili sauce may be added. Mix together well, then chill for about 1/2 hour before serving. May be served with tortilla chips.

Tortilla Chips

Cut tortillas into four parts, fry until crisp. Sprinkle with salt if desired.

Chili Sauce

1 large can tomato sauce

1 small onion

1 clove garlic

1 tsp. salt

1/2 tsp. black pepper

2-3 chili peppers (optional)

Mix all ingredients in blender until smooth sauce consistency. Serve on toquitos, combine in guacamole. Eat on chips.

Addendum

Soul Food Recipes

Fried Chicken

4 heaping tbsp. flour

3/4 cup milk

2 eggs

1 1/2 tsp. salt

1/2 tsp. pepper

1/2 tsp. garlic power

1/2 tsp. celery salt

1/2 tsp. paprika

1 tbsp. sugar

Mix flour with all spices, then add milk to flour mixture gradually making a paste. Beat eggs, with fork and add flour mixture. Dip chicken in above mixture then roll in dry flour and fry on medium heat in 2 cups vegetable oil (approx.) and 2 sticks margarine. Don't fry too fast, about medium heat on a larger burner on an electric stove. Let chicken brown very well on bottom side, turn and brown on the other side. Chicken should take approximately 45 minutes to complete. To reuse batter, freeze remainder. Strain grease through cloth and reuse. Eggs, milk and sugar may be omitted from the above recipe. After dipping chicken into the flour mixture, fry in hot skillet. Takes about 20 minutes.

Collard Greens

2 lbs. chicken neckbones

4 bunches collard greens

2 tbsp. of bacon drippings

Dash tabasco sauce

salt and pepper

Boil neckbones until tender, remove from pot. Add well washed greens that have been chopped. Cook over low flame until the greens are done. Add bacon fat and season to taste. Greens should be cooked uncovered and almost at a full boil so that you end up with only a small amount of "likker". This can be poured over the greens before serving.

Soul Food Recipes

Sweet Corn

2 large ears of corn

1 cup milk

2 tbsp. butter

1 1/2 tbsp. flour

salt and pepper

Cut corn from the cob. Mix with milk, butter, salt and pepper.
Slowly stir in flour. Cook over low heat until gravy thickens and
corn is cooked.

Hash Brown Potatoes

1 lb. salt pork

2 cups cold boiled potatoes, sliced

1/8 tsp. pepper

Fry fat out of salt pork, remove scraps. There should be 1/3 cup
of fat remaining. Mix the boiled potatoes with fat; add pepper and
salt. Fry, stirring occasionally until lightly browned.

Corn Bread

1 cup corn meal

1 cup flour

2 tbsp. sugar or more to taste

1 tbsp. baking power

1 tsp. salt

1/3 cup melted shortening

1 egg

1 cup milk

Combine dry ingredients and mix well. Add milk and blend. Add
egg and mix. Add melted oil and blend (melt oil in pan to be used
for baking bread). Bake in 8" square pan in hot oven 400 degrees
for 25 minutes or until brown.

Addendum

Soul Food Recipe

Sweet Potato Pie

1 pie crust (see below)

1 1/2 cups cooked, mashed yams

1/2 tsp. salt

1/2 cup brown sugar

1/4 tsp. cinnamon

2 eggs, well beaten

3/4 cup milk

1 tbsp. melted butter

Prepare crust and chill. Combine yams, brown sugar, salt, and cinnamon in bowl. Mix together eggs, milk, butter and stir into yam mixture thoroughly. Pour into chilled crust and bake in preheat oven to 400 degrees and bake for 45 minutes or until knife comes out dry when inserted in center.

Pie Crust

1 cup sifted all purpose flour

1/3 cup shortening

1/2 tsp. salt

3 tbsp. cold water

Sift flour and salt together. Cut in shortening with fork until the size of small peas. Sprinkle water over mixture. Form into smooth ball after tossing with fork. Roll out to fit 8" pie pan and chill.

Chitterlings

Clean and wash chitterlings first in sink. Place the chitterlings in a pot big enough to handle them. Add salt and pepper to add flavor. Put in 1 - 2 chopped onions. Also, lemon juice can be added if desired. Let cook for 2 - 4 hours. (Chitterlings can be served boiled or after boiling, pan fry with butter and onions.) If you get them fresh from a meat market the smell can be horrendous, so be sure to clean them in a well ventilated area. Although the smell is not quite as bad when purchased pre-packaged from a store, you will still need to remove much of the fat. Here is a handy way how:

Soul Food Recipes

Place them in a sink and pour boiling water on them. Cut into short pieces and place in a container of warm water. After they are all cut up wash them in warm water. At this point don't worry about the fat. It will melt off later. Place the now washed "chittlins" into a large pot. Add cold water and a tablespoon of salt. Cook the "chittlins" until they are hot (but don't boil them). Remove from heat. Use a scoop with holes and douse them, a few at a time in hot water and drain. The fat should stay in the hot water. After they all have been drained put in a pot with cold water, cover and cook slowly; add spices if you like. When they are good and tender add a cup of vinegar, stir and simmer 5 - 10 minutes. Some people prefer to fry them at this point. Serve with corn bread, cole slaw, black eyed peas and kool-aid and you have got yourself a real soul food meal.

Addendum

Chinese Food Recipes

Fried Rice

3-4 cups pre-cooked rice

4 tbsp oil

2 medium onions

1 cup of bean sprouts

3 eggs

1 tsp salt

1 tbsp soy sauce

Beat the eggs and cut up onions. Preheat pan and then add oil and heat. Pour in eggs. When half cooked set aside add rice and stir fry rapidly mixing the eggs into rice. Add onions, bean sprouts and any other partially cooked vegetables you like. Stir fry together add salt and soy sauce. Add 1/4 lb. of finely cut cooked meat (chicken, beef, pork, shrimp, etc.).

Egg Drop Soup

4 cups chicken stock

2 tbsp corn starch

1/4 tsp salt

3 drops sesame oil

1/4 tsp soy sauce

1 sliced onion minced fine

1 egg lightly beaten

Mix all of the items except the onion and egg and let boil. When mixture starts to boil, add egg and stir with a fork to break the egg into shreds. Add onions, turn off heat once the egg is set, about 1 or 2 minutes.

Chinese Food Recipes

Stir Fried Spinach

2 lbs. fresh spinach.

1 tbsp peanut oil

1/2 tsp salt

Wash spinach and remove stalks. Cut leaves into 1" squares. Heat peanut oil then add spinach and stir fry for 2 minutes. Then it is ready to eat.

Addendum

Recipe Books

> Your library should have numerous books on ethnic cooking. To select your own menus we refer you to the following books:

Soul Food

Southern Living, Cooking Across the South. Lillian Bertram Marshall. Oxmoor House, Inc., Birmingham, 1980.
Features a collection of favorite recipes from fifteen southern states.

Down Home Southern Cooking. LaMont Burns, Doubleday and Company, Inc., Garden City, NY, 1987.
Written by the owner of a barbeque restaurant, the author traces his culinary talents back to the slave kitchen of his great grandmother. *"Down Home Cooking"* features his secrets of herbs and spices in preparing soul food.

Native American Food

Pueblo Indian Cookbook. Compiled and edited by Phyllis Huges, Museum of New Mexico Press, 1972.
Includes recipes from the Pueblos of the American Southwest.

The Art of American Indian Cooking. Yeffe Kimball and Jean Anderson, Doubleday and Company, Inc., Garden City, NY, 1965.
Contains nearly 200 historic and authentic American Indian recipes.

Mexican Food

Mexican Cookbook. Editors of Sunset Books and Sunset Magazine, Lane Publishing Co., Menlo Park, CA, 1977.
Features over 200 recipes of Mexican cuisine.

Mexican American Plain Cooking. Bruce King, Nelson-Hall, Chicago, IL, 1982.
In addition to hundreds of recipes, this cookbook includes easy to follow cooking techniques.

Chinese Food

The Step By Step Chinese Cookbook. Georges Spunt, Thomas Y. Crowell Company, NY 1973.
Covers techniques of preparing Chinese food the way it is done in China.

The Complete Chinese Cookbook. CFW Publications Limited, Hong Kong, 1982.
Includes over 500 authentic recipes from China.

About the Author

-- "nothing like getting people together in the great outdoors."

Charles "Chuck" Taylor evolved into publishing. After presenting several workshops at national conferences people would consistently write for additional materials and information that could help them in their programming efforts. Chuck would respond to each letter pulling bits and pieces together from his files. As the requests increased he realized that a better system had to be developed to disseminate the different types of requests.

As a result he founded a national newsletter that eventually became a newspaper called the National Minority Campus Chronicle. This publication proved to be an effective way to network and share information on a regular basis. Shortly after its dissemination Dr. Taylor began publishing a series of pamphlets on specific topic areas.

Today he is in the business of publishing full length books that attempt to look at minority student services, human relations and cultural pluralism from a comprehensive perspective. He also conducts seminars and workshops related to the above topics throughout the country. He loves to facilitate cultural retreats and is fast becoming a "retreat guru".

Minority students services and human relations is nothing new to Dr. Taylor. He has been involved in these areas for over a decade. Charles has served as director of a Multicultural Education Center, as an academic advisor, as director of Human Relations for the Madison, Wisconsin Public School System, as Acting Vice Chancellor for Academic Support Services, as director of a TRIO program and similar positions during his illustrious career.

Dr. Taylor received his B.S. from Southeast Missouri State University, his M.S. from the University of Oregon and his Phd in Curriculum and Instruction - (Educational Technology) at the University of Wisconsin - Madison.

Addendum

Related Books of Interest

Effective Ways to Recruit and Retain Minority Students

This publication is a must for universities and colleges. It provides a coordinated approach to recruiting and retaining minority students, speaks to factors that create retention problems, features successful programs from around the country and lists dozens of ideas you can implement on your campus immediately. ($29.95)

How To Sponsor a Minority Cultural Retreat

Looking for ways to break down racial barriers and ways to get minority and white students to interact, then this book is for you. This handbook shows you step by step how to conduct a retreat and is filled with activities to ensure your retreat's success. ($24.95)

Guide to Multicultural Resources (1989-90 edition)

The guide is a comprehensive collection of programs, organizations, businesses, services and related information from Black, Hispanic, American Indian and Asian communities. Anyone wishing to network with the minority community should have this book. Includes names, addresses and phone numbers of hundreds of entries. ($58.00)

The Handbook of Minority Student Services

Everything students, faculty and administrators need to establish successful minority programs on campus. A necessary book for student services staff and campus planners. ($49.95)

To order any of the above books add $3.50 shipping and handling and mail check or money order to:

Praxis Publications
P.O. Box 9869
Madison, WI 53715

For additional information call: 608/244-5633